PAULINE KELLY

This book is dedicated to my first teachers in St Agnes National School Crumlin, who taught me to write clearly, read for pleasure and enjoy reciting poetry by heart. –P.K.

Gill Education
Hume Avenue
Park West
Dublin 12

www.gilleducation.ie

Gill Education is an imprint of M.H. Gill & Co.

ISBN: 9780717180998

Design and layout: Mike Connor Design & Illustration

'Pull Like A Dog', Tuesday 27th December, reproduced by kind permission of presspack.rte.ie.

'Mushrooms' by Sylvia Plath, from *Collected Poems* by Sylvia Plath, published by Faber and Faber Ltd, 2002.

Extracts from 'Stopping by Woods on a Snowy Evening', From Collected Poems by Robert Frost. Published by Vintage Classics. Reprinted by permission of The Random House Group Limited. © 1930.

For permission to reproduce photographs, the author and publisher gratefully acknowledge the following:

© Alamy: 26, 37, 43, 60, 64, 142; © AP/REX/Shutterstock: 34; Courtesy of Basketball Ireland: 166; Courtesy of Carnival Film & Television Limited: 145; Courtesy of Central Statistics Office: 118, 139; © David Fitzgerald/Sportsfile: 31; © DELIL SOULEIMAN/AFP/ Getty Images: 128; © Lebrecht Music & Arts: 65; Courtesy of NASA: 56; © Paul Sharp/SHARPPIX: 40.

The author and publisher have made every effort to trace all copyright holders, but if any have been inadvertently overlooked we would be pleased to make the necessary arrangement at the first opportunity.

CONTENTS

What this Examination is About

The final examination in English tests what you know, understand and are able to do in **Oral Language**, **Reading** and **Writing**.

The skills to be examined are stated in **three sets of Learning Outcomes**.

Definition

A **Learning Outcome** describes what a student knows, understands, or is able to do in a final examination.

1. What do the ORAL LANGUAGE Learning Outcomes say?

When you read or listen to a spoken text, which might be a speech, poem, drama, talk, radio or digital broadcast, etc. you should be able to:

- Explain what it's about.
- Point out the qualities that catch and hold the attention of listeners.
- Show that the speaker's tone, language and style reflect his or her purpose, the time and setting, and the audience of listeners or viewers.
- Describe the impact that the spoken words would have on listeners or viewers.

2. What do the READING Learning Outcomes say?

When you are given a passage to read, you should be able to:

- Show understanding of the ideas; make connections with what you already know; learn from the piece you have read, enjoy it, question it and judge its qualities.
- Use the proper terms for drama, film, fiction, poetry or for a digital text.
- Write about character, dialogue, setting, action, plot, etc.
- Choose and analyse a key moment.
- Point out and appreciate different forms of language, e.g. the rich language of poetry; the language of film; the language of formal documents, the superlative language of advertisers or promoters; the factual language of news broadcasts etc.
- Comment on choice of words, turns of phrase, striking images, etc.
- Compare and contrast texts.

3. What do the WRITING Learning Outcomes say?

When you are asked to write, you should be able to:

- Write correctly for any purpose, e.g. explain, imagine, narrate, persuade, argue, comment on a text or picture, etc.
- Use appropriate vocabulary, register, tone or style depending on your purpose and audience.
- Proofread and edit your writing to make it clear and correct.
- Spell, punctuate and paragraph correctly.
- Write intelligently about the texts you have studied and respond imaginatively to them.

- In your studied texts, write about key moments, about character(s), important events, turning points, moments that were especially moving, funny or sad etc.
- Show that, through regular writing, you have developed your own writing style. You take pleasure in writing well. You have good command of vocabulary, sentence structure and grammar.

In each examination, page 1 of the paper presents a short list of the aspects of the Learning Outcomes that have been selected for testing in that year. Here are some examples:

Appreciating audience and register

Reading comprehension strategies

Appreciating language

Responding to texts

Reading to analyse and evaluate

Responding to studied texts

Showing critical appreciation

Reading for comparison

Appreciating character, setting, story and action

Engaging in the writing process

Reading to understand – Shakespearean drama

Some Practical Advice

There are 180 marks in total. The sections vary from year to year. The number of sections, the headings taken from the learning outcomes, and the allocation of marks are different from year to year.

Every examination has a **THEME.**

Highlight the theme on page 1 and look for opportunities to mention it in your answers,

e.g. The theme of this examination paper is
Celebration / Mystery / Courage / Magic / War / Friendship etc.

Timing

You have **120 minutes** in which to answer all questions. Your first task is to plan the time so that you have completed all sections at the end of the 120 minutes.

- On page 1 of the paper, you will be given timing guidelines a few lines below the headings, e.g. You should spend about 25 minutes on Section A..
- Highlight these times and use the **first five minutes** to plan your timing.
- On the right-hand side of the sections, write the **starting time** for each section.
- Stick to these times to keep yourself on track. In this way, you will finish every question in **120 minutes**.

			Start time
Section A Reading to analyse and evaluate	35 marks	2 questions	9.35
Section B Showing critical appreciation	45 marks	2 questions	10.00
Section C Appreciating character, story, setting, action	75 marks	5 questions	10.30
Section D Engaging in the writing process	25 marks	1 question	11.15

The minutes add up to 115. This allows only the first five minutes to work out the start times for each question.

You need to start every question on time so that you will have time for the final question. In a two-hour examination, time is tight!

Spelling and punctuation

How many marks will I lose for bad **spelling** and **punctuation**?

You may lose up to 10% of the marks for an answer if your spelling and punctuation are not at Higher Level standard. One or two mistakes will not be penalised. The examiner will take it into account if you misspelt some ambitious vocabulary, but carelessly repeated common errors are not acceptable. Eliminate your errors by working on the **Common Errors** section of this book (see page 222).

Practise the PIE method in your paragraphing

You will frequently be reminded that a good examination answer is composed of well-structured paragraphs.

In each paragraph you write, you should try to apply the 'PIE' method.

The acronym PIE stands for

Point **Illustrate** **Explain**

This means that you should (1) make your POINT, (2) ILLUSTRATE the point you've made with a quotation or reference to the text, and then (3) EXPLAIN your point.

Before the examination

Prepare your key scenes and your quotations

You should know the key scenes/moments in your **novels**, **plays**, **short stories** and **film** so well that you can clearly see and hear them running like little movies in your head. In the examination, visualise these scenes and refer to them in detail.

How do I recognise a key scene or moment? ✔

A key scene will make a special impression and capture your full attention. It may develop the plot, highlight the theme, shed light on character(s) or create an unforgettable moment or atmosphere. ✔

Read and reread those memorable **key scenes** in the days before the examination. Learn quotations from them. Be able to say them correctly without looking at your book. **Quotations** back up your points. They help you to argue, illustrate and develop the points you make. Note that you must **quote accurately**.

Your studied poems

Poems that have **rich themes**, **interesting use of language**, **impressive techniques** and **strong imagery** will serve you well in the examination. Your selection should give you many examples of poetic techniques, different people and places, strong emotions, etc. Read these chosen poems aloud and imagine them so often that you can run through the stanzas in your head. Be able to write **quotations** from your special poems; opening lines, closing lines, enjoyable or memorable lines, etc.

During the examination

	I always do this	I need to improve this
• Highlight the **theme** given on page 1 of the paper.		
• Figure out your **start** times for each question.		
• Highlight the **key words** in every question.		
• Know how many things you are being asked to do before you begin to write your answer (answering only **part** of the question is one of the most common ways to lose marks in the examination).		
• Highlight the **number of marks** given at the top of each question within the sections – higher marked answers get more minutes.		
• **Short, clear, precise sentences** communicate your ideas better than long, rambling sentences (especially when starting paragraphs).		
• Start a **new paragraph** for a **new point**.		
• **Back up** every point with **evidence**.		
• Place **accurate quotations** between inverted commas.		
• Spell names of **characters**, **texts** and **authors** correctly.		
• Place **titles** of texts between inverted commas.		

An important point about your studied Shakespeare

Be clear on differences between the film version and the stage play. A film of your play is an excellent support to your learning, and you may refer to a moment that you especially liked in the film, but the examiner is giving marks for knowledge of the **play written by Shakespeare**, not the **film** created by a modern film director.

Use the space provided correctly

Write your answers neatly and clearly in black pen within the spaces provided:

At the end of each section, there is an extra page called 'Additional Writing Space'. You use it if you need more than the space provided directly below the question(s). If you write on this extra page, you MUST clearly write the question number and the part of the question that you are answering, for example:

Additional Writing Space. Label all work clearly with the question number and part.

Question 2 part (b)

Finally, at the very end of the full paper, more pages are given. Here, you must label each answer with the section, the number of the question and the part of the question, for example:

Question number	Write the question numbers in the left-hand margin
Section A, Question 1, Part (a)	

Additional space and extra pages are not provided in this book. If you need additional space for an answer, use your copybook or lined paper.

This book aims to create the confident examination writer, a strong and skilful higher level candidate.

Take a few moments to write some short bullet points for 1 and 2 below.

Your points at 3 will be written when you have completed the work in the book.

1. The strengths I bring to this exam are:

- ______________________________

2. Here are some things I would like to improve on:

- ______________________________

3. These are the skills that I have achieved by working through this book:

- ______________________________

Test Your Critical Vocabulary

Introduction

Students should be able to:

Use an appropriate critical vocabulary when responding to literary texts.

(Final Examination Requirement: English Specification, 14)

This means that you should know, understand and be able to use the special vocabulary of plays, films, fiction and poetry.

> **Tip**
> An answer that uses the correct critical terms will be highly rewarded.

This is normal learning for any specialist. For example, a mechanic uses the correct terms for every part of an engine, *catalyst*, *driveshafts*, etc.; a doctor uses the correct terms for body parts, *hallux*, *lymph nodes*, etc.; a football coach talks about *possession*, the *defensive wall*, or the *six-yard box*.

As a literary critic, you should be able to identify a *sonnet*, a *sub-plot*, a *soliloquy*, a *prologue*; speak about *character*, *narrator*, *twist in the tale*, *setting*, *stagecraft*, *props*, *gesture* and *dialogue*; refer by their proper names to the many techniques used by a novelist, poet, playwright, film director, documentary maker, etc.

Write a definition of five critical terms that have appeared in examination papers to date.

1. Aside ______________________________

   ____

2. Assonance ______________________________

   ____

3. Blank verse ______________________________

   ____

4. Soliloquy ______________________________

   ____

5. Setting ______________________________

   ____

My score out of **20** is ______.

Start practising writing clear, legible sentences in black pen, fitted neatly into these lines, as you will have to do in the final examination.

General Terms and Vocabulary

The following exercise will guide you in the correct spelling of general terms used in writing about short stories, novels, plays, films or poems.

There are **15** terms to be completed.

Score **2** marks for each correct answer. **30** gives you full marks.

Tip

Look away from your book and recite the correct spelling as you complete each word!

1. The people in a play, novel, film or short story are called

C			R						S

2. The time and place in which a story is set is called the

S					N	G

3. The correct term for the clothes that actors wear in a play or film is

C						

4. The correct term for a story in a play, novel or film is

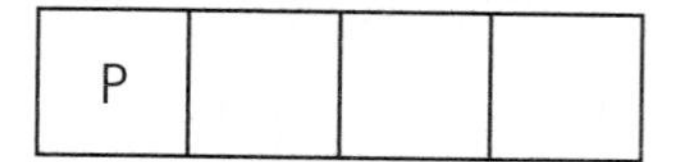

5. Another word for the main character in a play, novel, short story or film is

P					G					T

6. The plays of Shakespeare are divided into sections called

A			S

and

S					S

7. A person who writes plays is called a

P				W					T

or a

D			M	A			S	

8. A person who writes novels is called a

N						S	T

9. A person who creates a film or a stage performance and tells actors what to do on stage or in filming is called a

D							R

10. Alliteration, personification and onomatopoeia are all examples of poetic

T		C				Q		E

11. A very long speech, spoken without interruption by one person on a stage or in a film is called a

M		N		L		G		E

12. A film or television or radio programme that provides a factual report on a particular subject is called a

D		C		M					R	Y

13. A short passage taken from a poem, play or novel is called an

E			R			T

14. An alphabetical list of unusual or difficult words at the back of a book, giving explanations of what the words mean.

G	L			S		R	Y

15. A story of someone's life, written by someone else

B			G					Y

My total score out of **30** is ______.

Poetry

Poets use language in a special way that is pleasing to the ear, appealing to the senses and striking to the emotions.

Poets use many **techniques** as part of their special way with words. Sometimes the poet will repeat letters that start words placed close together (**alliteration**; example: ____), or perhaps repeat vowel sounds so you hear rhyme within the line (**assonance**; example: ____). Assonance and alliteration are pleasing to the ear and can make the lines in a poem move along rhythmically. Assonance is also called **internal rhyme**.

> **Definition**
>
> A **poetic technique** is an imaginative use of words that adds energy, colour, sound effects, originality, pleasure, excitement, beauty, surprise, deep meaning or emotion, or other richness to the poem.

The feeling of an unstoppable advance movement can be achieved by using **run-on lines** (also called **enjambment**; example: ____ ____) where the reader is carried forward without punctuation from one line or from one stanza to the next.

Personification (giving human qualities to animals or things; example: ____ ____) can also be used to powerful effect. In Sylvia Plath's 'Mushrooms', on the following page, mushrooms are personified, as if they were humans with specific body parts; with hopes, feelings, strategies and ambitions; doing human things like gasping for air, climbing, heaving, putting a foot in a door.

If you are asked about **tone**, you should **speak** the poem and listen to your tone of voice. If you dramatically act out the words and their meaning, you will read some lines softly and others loudly, some slowly and some quickly, some gently and some with a sinister edge to your voice, etc. Try doing all of this by reading 'Mushrooms' aloud, acting out the lines as if you were telling a ghost story.

Imagery is where a picture or perhaps a sound forms in your mind as you read the words. An image can pack a lot of meaning, emotion and ideas into a few words.

Here is an example of a paragraph that uses the PIE method:

'Mushrooms' is a poem packed with powerful images that tell a strange story. 'Soft fists ... heaving the needles' tells you that these fists seem gentle but are really mighty, and willing to endure suffering and pain on their journey. 'Crumbs of shadow' suggests tough survivors who persist on little or nothing. The repeated line 'So many of us!' is a scary image of an unstoppable force. 'Our foot's in the door', in my opinion, is the best image because it is threatening and sinister. It declares softly, confidently, firmly that they are sly and determined and should be feared.

> **Tip**
>
> 
>
>
> Notice the use of PIE (**P**oint, **I**llustration, **E**xplanation). The leader sentence makes the point about powerful, vivid imagery. The sentences that follow develop that point with supporting illustration and explanation.

A note on quotation in the examination

You will not be rewarded for incorrect quotes. Learn a selection of quotes from each of your studied poems. This will become your store of supporting evidence in the examination.

Mushrooms

Overnight, very
Whitely, discreetly,
Very quietly

Our toes, our noses
Take hold on the loam,
Acquire the air.

Nobody sees us,
Stops us, betrays us;
The small grains make room.

Soft fists insist on
Heaving the needles,
The leafy bedding,

Even the paving.
Our hammers, our rams,
Earless and eyeless,

Perfectly voiceless,
Widen the crannies,
Shoulder through holes. We

Diet on water,
On crumbs of shadow,
Bland-mannered, asking

Little or nothing.
So many of us!
So many of us!

We are shelves, we are
Tables, we are meek,
We are edible,

Nudgers and shovers
In spite of ourselves.
Our kind multiplies:

We shall by morning
Inherit the earth.
Our foot's in the door.

Sylvia Plath

Identify **one** example of each of the following poetic techniques used by Sylvia Plath in 'Mushrooms':

Allusion: when an author refers to people, places or events in another text, e.g. a biblical allusion.

____

____

Assonance/internal rhyme: repetition of vowel sounds within words close together.

____

____

Enjambment: a line that continues to the next line without a pause or grammatical break.

____

____

Imagery: language that presents visual or sensory pictures or comparisons.

____

____

Personification: giving human thoughts, features or emotions to animals or things.

____

____

Examples of critical vocabulary used in your studied poems

There are **15** multiple choice questions.

Score **2** marks for each multiple choice answer you get correct, making a total of **30**.

Score a further **6** marks for each **complete** answer in the second part of the question, i.e. the title and author of a poem, and, where it is asked for, an example from that poem. **15*6** will give you a further **90** marks.

The full total will be **120** marks.

Tip

As you write the title of each poem (between inverted commas) and the name of the poet, learn the correct spelling in each case so that you become exam-ready.

1. A poet's skilful or imaginative way of using language is called a
   A. Special effect
   B. Technique
   C. Climax

   Write the title and author of a poem you have read that uses this special language.

Name the poem	Name the poet

2. When words imitate the sound being described, this is called
   A. Personification
   B. Simile
   C. Onomatopoeia

   Write an example of this technique from a poem you have read.

' ______________________________
______________________________ '

Name the poem	Name the poet

3. When several words in a line begin with the same letter, this is called
   A. Metaphor
   B. Alliteration
   C. Imagery

   Write an example of this technique from a poem you have read.

' ______________________________
______________________________ '

Name the poem	Name the poet

4. When vowel sounds are repeated in a line, this is called
   A. Alliteration
   B. Symbol
   C. Assonance

   Write an example of this technique from a poem you have read.

‘ ______________________________ ’	
Name the poem	Name the poet

5. When two things are compared with the word 'like' or 'as', this is called
   A. Simile
   B. Onomatopoeia
   C. Rhyme

   Write an example of this technique from a poem you have read.

‘ ______________________________ ’	
Name the poem	Name the poet

6. An imaginative comparison that does not use 'like' or 'as' is called a
   A. Rhythm
   B. Metaphor
   C. Alliteration

   Write an example of this technique from a poem you have read.

‘ ______________________________ ’	
Name the poem	Name the poet

7. When an object or animal is spoken about as if it had human feelings, this is called
   A. Tone
   B. Personification
   C. Theme

   Write an example of this technique from a poem you have read.

' ______________________________ ______________________________ '	
Name the poem	Name the poet

8. The central idea or message in a poem is called the
   A. Image
   B. Theme
   C. Mood

An example of a ______________ in a poem I have read is ______________________________ ______________________________	
Name the poem	Name the poet

9. The repetitive beat or metre in a poem is called
   A. Rhyme
   B. Rhythm
   C. Refrain

   Write an example of this technique that you particularly enjoyed in a poem you have read.

' ______________________________ ______________________________ '	
Name the poem	Name the poet

Tip

Make a list of the poems that are giving you examples of techniques in these answers. This list can start a collection of **poems for special study** that you will read over the night before the examination.

10. A poem of 14 lines with a special rhyme scheme is called a
   A. Ballad
   B. Lyric
   C. Sonnet

   Write the title and author of one of these poems that you have read.

Name the poem	Name the poet

11. A poem that attacks its subject by making it look ridiculous is called a
   A. Sonnet
   B. Satire
   C. Limerick

   Write the title and author of one of these poems that you have read.

Name the poem	Name the poet

12. An exaggerated statement that is not meant to be taken literally is called
   A. Hyperbole
   B. Assonance
   C. A factual statement

   Write an example of this technique from a poem you have read.

‘ ______________________________

______________________________ ’

Name the poem	Name the poet

13. When you have to read on to the next line in the poem to complete the meaning, this is called
   A. Enjambment
   B. Alliteration
   C. Hyperbole

   Write an example of this technique from a poem you have read.

‘ ______________________________

______________________________ ’

Name the poem	Name the poet

14. When there is a play on words, i.e. a word is used that can have two different meanings, this is called
    A. Parody
    B. Plot
    C. Pun

    Write an example of this technique from a poem you have read.

' ____ ____ '	
Name the poem	Name the poet

15. A long poem that tells a heroic story about heroes or gods in the past is called
    A. A lullaby
    B. An epic
    C. A lyric

    Can you name a long poem that tells a heroic story about heroes or gods in the past?

Name the poem	Name the poet

My multiple choice score out of **30** is ______.

My score out of **90** for poem titles, poets and examples is ______.

My total score out of **120** is ______.

More poetic terms – Forms of poems and poetic techniques

Fill in the gaps with the correct poetic term.

There are **15** terms to be completed.

Score **2** marks for each correct answer to make a total of **30**.

1. 'Shall I compare thee to a summer's day' is a famous ______________________ by Shakespeare.
2. 'I hear lake water lapping with low sounds' and 'His foxy face was frantic as he flew' are examples of ______________________.
3. 'There was an old man with a beard' by Edward Lear is a type of poem called a ______________________.
4. 'Whack, ting, splosh, swish flap-flip, crackle, snicker-snack' are examples of ______________________.
5. 'I fall upon the thorns of life, I bleed' is an example of ______________________.

6. 'Ears like bombs and teeth like splinters' and 'our hands sticky as Bluebeard's' are examples of ______________________________.

7. 'The wind howled, the lightning danced' and 'The lava swallowed the village' are examples of ______________________________.

8. 'Peter Piper picked a piece of pickled pepper' is an example of ______________________________ and ______________________________.

9. 'Nine bean-rows will I have there, a hive', 'Fire and ice' and 'with sickly single candle lit' are examples of ______________________________.

10. 'Pack up the moon and dismantle the sun', 'ten thousand saw I at a glance', and 'my bag weighs a ton' are examples of ______________________________.

11. 'The puffy-faced general guzzled and gulped in the best hotel' is an example of ______________________________ and ______________________________.

12. 'Next morning, I went into the room. Snowdrops
And candles soothed the bedside' is an example of ______________________________ and ______________________________.

13. 'The silence surged softly backward' is another example of ______________________________.

14. 'Love is patient, love is kind' is another example of ______________________________.

15. 'So long as men can breathe or eyes can see, / So long lives this, and this gives life to thee' is an example of a ______________________________ co______________________________t.

My score out of **30** is ______.

A poem for study

She Dwelt Among the Untrodden Ways

She dwelt among the untrodden ways
Beside the springs of Dove,
A Maid whom there were none to praise
And very few to love;

A violet by a mossy stone
Half hidden from the eye!
—Fair as a star, when only one
Is shining in the sky.

She lived unknown, and few could know
When Lucy ceased to be;
But she is in her grave, and, oh,
The difference to me!

William (?)

There are **10** multiple choice questions to be answered.

Score **2** marks for each correct answer to make a total of **20**.

In each case, write the letter corresponding to the correct answer in the box.

1. Lucy lived in
   A. A lively city
   B. A remote place in the country
   C. A well-known village

2. 'Untrodden' means
   A. Not walked on
   B. Unmissable
   C. Damp

3. 'A violet by a mossy stone' is an example of
   A. Metaphor
   B. Simile
   C. Alliteration

4. 'When Lucy ceased to be' is an example of
   A. Assonance
   B. Personification
   C. Alliteration

5. 'Half-hidden from the eye' is an example of
   A. Assonance
   B. Hyperbole
   C. Alliteration

6. 'Fair as a star' is an example of
   A. Metaphor
   B. Simile
   C. Alliteration

7. This poem is an example of
   A. A lyric
   B. An epic
   C. A satire

8. *abab cdcd efef* describes what in this poem?
   A. The rhythm
   B. The rhyme scheme
   C. The tone

9. The author of this poem is
   A. William Shakespeare
   B. William Wordsworth
   C. William Butler Yeats

10. Which one of these Williams is not a poet?
    A. William Blake
    B. Billy (William) Collins
    C. William Kavanagh

My score out of **20** is ______.

Drama

In each case, write the letter corresponding to the answer in the box.

A. There are **10** multiple choice questions to be answered.

Score **2** marks for each correct answer to make a total of **20**.

1. The part of a theatre in which the audience sits to watch the performance is called the
   A. Backstage
   B. Foyer
   C. Auditorium

2. The painted piece of material hung at the back of the stage as a background is called a
   A. Pit
   B. Prop
   C. Backdrop

3. Conversations between characters in a play are called
   A. Discussions
   B. Dialogues
   C. Monologues

4. The parts of the script in a play that tell the actors how they are to move or to speak their lines are called
   A. Exits
   B. Stage directions
   C. Scenes

5. The most dramatic and exciting moment or event in a play is called the
   A. Dénouement
   B. Theme
   C. Climax

6. This adjective describes characters who play smaller parts in a play.
   A. Major
   B. Minor
   C. Central

7. A small but meaningful movement made by an actor that conveys emotion without words is called a
   A. Special effect
   B. Prop
   C. Gesture

8. The feeling of excitement, fear or worry that something unexpected, frightening or strange is about to happen is called
   A. Climax
   B. Suspense
   C. Action

9. A sub-plot is
   A. A separate story that runs parallel to the main story
   B. A plot that is sub-standard
   C. A story that turns out in an unexpected way

10. Which definition best fits the word 'cliffhanger'?
    A. A dramatic and exciting ending to a scene, leaving the audience in suspense about what might happen next
    B. An unusual piece of scenery used
    C. When one of the characters is in extreme danger

☐

My score out of **20** is ______.

B. Complete the following dramatic terms. Score **2** marks for each correct answer to make a total of **20**.

1. The struggle, fight or disagreement between characters or between a character and the world in which s/he lives is called

C			F				T

2. This word is used to describe an unexpected turn of events in a play.

T				T

3. Another word used for the storyline or plot is the

N		R			T			E

4. A striking difference between two elements, e.g. characters, costumes, places, etc., which is used for dramatic effect is called

C		N				S	T

5. Classical drama is from the past, so what word is used for drama set in the present day?

C		N			M	P				R	Y

6. A minor plot running parallel to the main plot is called a

S			-				T

7. The building in which plays are performed is called a

T				T		E

8. The adjective made from the noun Shakespeare is

S	H		K		S				R			N

9. The hanging or design at the back of the stage is called the

B			K				P

10. The playwright's instructions for how actors should move or speak lines are called

S				E

D		R							S

My score out of **20** is ______.

Film

There are **7** multiple choice questions to be answered.

There are **8** words to be completed.

Score **2** marks for each correct answer to make a total of **30**.

1. A person whose voice tells the story in a film is called the
   A. Director
   B. Prompter
   C. Narrator ☐

2. The different kinds of film, e.g. comedies, musicals, tragedies, fantasy, sci-fi, etc., are called
   A. Genres
   B. Special effects
   C. Features ☐

3. The part of a film which shows events that occurred before the action in the film is called
   A. Flashback
   B. Storyline
   C. Epilogue ☐

4. An audio or film production that gives a factual report about a particular subject, often including interviews, documents and pictures is called a
   A. Video
   B. Drama
   C. Documentary ☐

5. The arrangement of everything that appears in a film frame – i.e. actors, lighting, décor, props, costume – is called
   A. Mise-en-scène
   B. Wide-angle shot
   C. Monologue ☐

6. The method of making films with pictures or models that appear to speak, act and move like people is called
   A. Special effects
   B. Animation
   C. Features ☐

7. The combination of recorded sounds and music for a film is called the
   A. Storyboard
   B. Musical score
   C. Soundtrack

☐

8. Emma Watson's ______________________ as Hermione in the *Harry Potter* films shot her to fame.

P			F		R					E

9. The opposite character to the hero in a film is the

		L	L			

10. The list of names shown at the beginning or end of the film is called the

C			D			S

11. Original music written specifically to accompany a film is called the film

			R	

12. This word describes the moment in the film music when it grows louder and more intense in order to create a sense of drama or excitement.

C			S				D	O

13. The correct term for the person who writes the music is

C		M				E	R

14. The positioning of the camera used to view a scene, e.g. from above or below, is called the camera

	N			E

15. A shot that puts the focus on a person's face is called a

			S		-		

My score out of **30** is ______.

Shakespearean Drama

There are **10** multiple choice questions.

Give yourself **2** marks for each answer, making a total of **20**.

1. Shakespeare's plays are divided into five of these, each having several smaller subsections.
   A. Scenes
   B. Sections
   C. Acts

2. A speech in which a character speaks an innermost thought to him or herself is called
   A. An aside
   B. A soliloquy
   C. An image

3. A remark spoken out loud and directed at the audience rather than at other characters on stage is called
   A. A soliloquy
   B. An aside
   C. A parody

4. The regular rhythm of Shakespeare's language in unrhymed lines is called
   A. Rhyming couplets
   B. Prose
   C. Blank verse

5. His lines are each composed of 10 syllables, organised in 5 pairs of a short syllable followed by a long syllable. This is called *iambic*
   A. Verse
   B. Rhythm
   C. Pentameter

6. A Shakespearean play that tells the story of the downfall and death of a heroic character is called a
   A. History
   B. Comedy
   C. Tragedy

7. A Shakespearean play that tells a story about romance, and has many twists and turns, usually ending in marriage in the closing scene, is called a
   A. History
   B. Comedy
   C. Tragedy

8. 'For never was a story of more woe / Than this of Juliet and her Romeo' is an example of
   A. Prose
   B. A rhyming couplet
   C. Monologue

9. When Romeo says, 'you have dancing shoes / With nimble soles: I have a soul of lead,' this is an example of a
   A. Rhyming couplet
   B. Pun
   C. Parody

10. When a Shakespearean character speaks lines which are understood in a double sense by the audience, but not by the character, this is called ______________________________. This term is also used when events turn out to be the very opposite of what might have been expected.
   A. Satire
   B. Hyperbole
   C. Irony

My score out of **20** is ______.

Novel and Short Story

In each case, write the letter corresponding to the answer in the box.

There are **10** multiple choice questions to be answered.

Give yourself **2** marks for each correct answer, making a total of **20**.

1. The time and place in which the story happens is called the
   A. Theme
   B. Flashback
   C. Setting

2. A book that contains a selection of short stories by different authors is called an
   A. Encyclopaedia
   B. Anthology
   C. Obituary

3. Another word for the main or central character is the
   A. Antagonist
   B. Protagonist
   C. Villain

4. The term for a particular kind of fiction, e.g. horror, crime, historical, romance, fantasy, is
   A. Genre
   B. Classics
   C. Dénouement

5. A story which is too long to be a short story and too short to be a novel is called
   A. An article
   B. A novella
   C. An essay

6. A book which continues the story of a previous book is called a
   A. Sequel
   B. Prequel
   C. Prologue

7. A short description of a book on the back cover which is intended to make people buy the book (e.g. 'a memorable, magical story that will touch your heart') is called a
   A. Blurb
   B. Epilogue
   C. Dedication

8. A short introduction, written either by the author or by someone else, at the beginning of a book is called a
   A. Preface
   B. Appendix
   C. Glossary

9. A great novel that continues to be read long after its author has died is called a
   A. Manuscript
   B. Hardback
   C. Classic

10. A novel such as George Orwell's *Animal Farm* or *1984* that 'sends up' or ridicules its subject while telling a story is called a
    A. Coming of age story
    B. Satire
    C. Autobiography

My score out of **20** is ______.

Narrative techniques in novels and short stories

Definition

A **narrative technique** is a method or strategy used by the storyteller to shape the story. It can engage the reader by adding richness, interest, pleasure, deep meaning or emotion to the text. For example, beginning a story with the phrase 'once upon a time' is a traditional narrative technique.

In each case, write the letter corresponding to the answer in the box.

There are **10** multiple choice questions to be answered.

Give yourself **2** marks for each correct answer, making a total of **20**.

1. The point in a story in which a crisis or issue reaches its moment of greatest intensity is called the
   A. Climax
   B. Plot
   C. Conflict

2. When a story ends with a sudden, unpredictable statement or event that shocks or surprises the reader, you call this ending
   A. The resolution
   B. A twist in the tale
   C. Tension

3. When the story is told by 'I', i.e. a character in the story, you call this
   A. Third person narration
   B. First person narration
   C. Monologue

4. When an author adds a short piece after the story has finished, perhaps telling you something that happened to characters after the novel ended, this is called an
   A. Addition
   B. Epilogue
   C. Afterthought

5. The use of small details or description in the early part of a story that will hint at later events or take on more meaning as the story unfolds is called
   A. Twist in the tale
   B. Foreshadowing
   C. Characterisation

6. A surprising contrast between what actually happens and what would have been expected to happen, or between what is said and what is really meant is called
   A. Tension
   B. Irony
   C. Satire

7. A dramatic or exciting ending to a chapter that leaves the reader in suspense and anxious to find out what happens next is called a
   A. Narrative
   B. Conflict
   C. Cliffhanger

8. A story, often containing animals, which tells some moral truth is called a
   A. Fable
   B. Suspense
   C. Plot

9. A reference to another story in a novel or a short story is called an
   A. Illusion
   B. Image
   C. Allusion

10. A series of novels telling the story of a family through several generations is called a
    A. Saga
    B. Satire
    C. Symbol

My score out of **20** is ______.

Non-Literary, Media and Digital Texts

In each case below, match the word to the correct definition.

There are **15** definitions to be matched.

Give yourself **3** marks for each correct answer, making a total of **45**.

Word
Homepage
Documentary
Tagline
Graphic novel
Word cloud
Frame
Blog
Tabloid
VLE
Broadsheet
Infographic
Audio text
Multi-modal text
Vlog
Navigation

Definition
A novel in comic-strip format
A compact-size popular newspaper, heavily illustrated with photographs and hyperbolic headlines, which prints sensational crime stories, short articles and celebrity gossip often using hyperbole
A large format newspaper, with long articles, which prints serious news stories and uses a wider vocabulary than tabloids
A visual learning environment in which learning materials can be accessed online
A text designed for listening
A radio or TV programme using pictures/interviews/ real events, to provide a factual report on a subject
A visual display of words used in a particular text or subject, in which the size of each word indicates its frequency or importance
A blog which includes video material
A regularly updated web page, often written by an individual or small group, in informal or conversational style
A diagram, often colourful, usually containing words and images, which lays out information in visual form
A single picture in a comic strip
A text which uses a variety of ways to communicate, e.g. spoken language, words, visuals, sounds, etc.
The first page you see on a website, usually laying out the contents of the site
How the user is helped to move from one page to another on a website
A catchphrase or slogan, often with the words placed next to the logo on a webpage

My score out of **45** is ______.

Add three more terms with the correct definitions:

Word	Definition
1.	
2.	
3.	

In the grid below, write ten definitions of special terms used in this section of the book.

Swap with your partner and ask him or her to fill in the correct term alongside your definition.

Definition	The correct term is
1.	
2.	
3.	
4.	
5.	
6.	
7.	
8.	
9.	
10.	

Short Sample Questions

Examination Skills

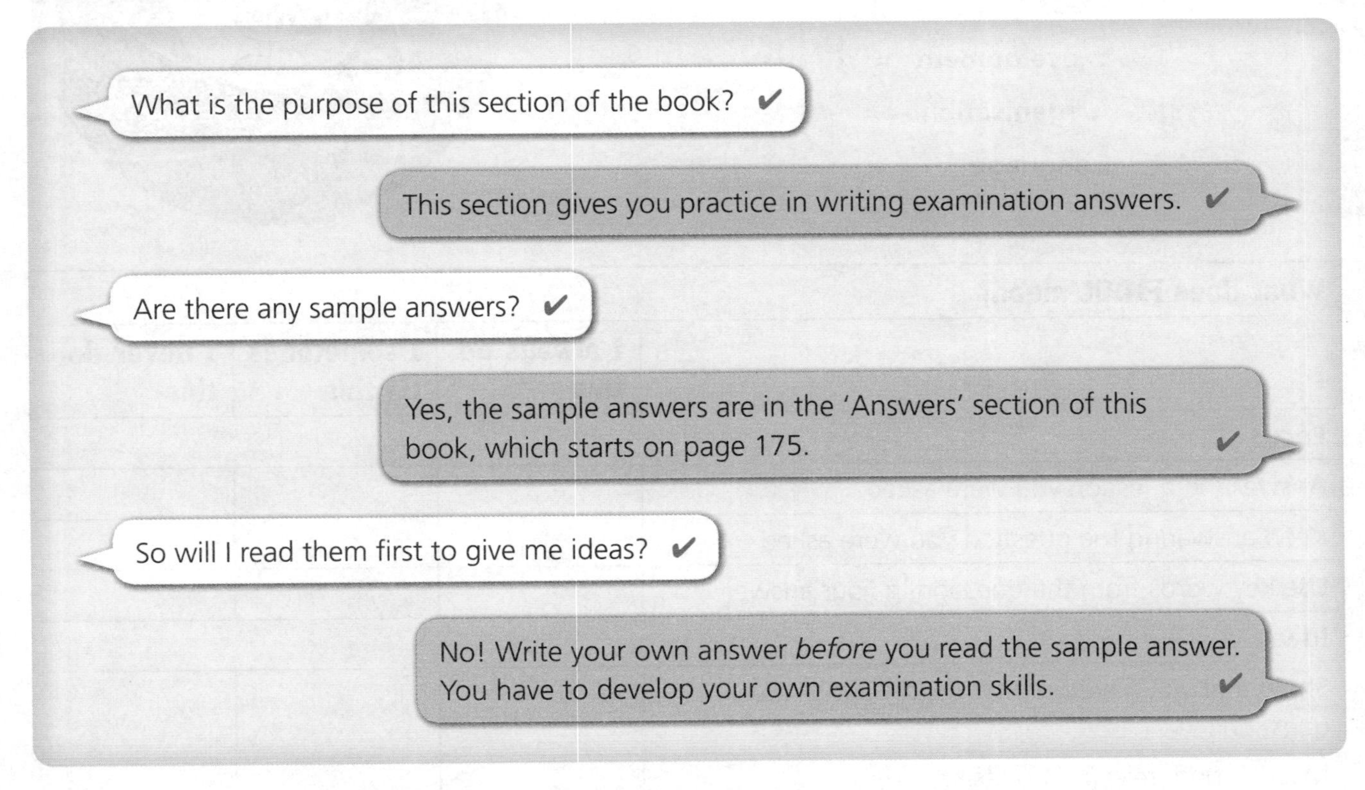

What two basic skills must I apply to an examination answer?

1. Answer the examination question *in full*, paying attention to everything you are asked to do. Do not leave out any part of the question.
2. Arrange your answer in a number of short paragraphs.

What other skills will help to raise my marks to high quality level?

3. Start with a strong, clear sentence that directly addresses the question.
4. Repeat key words from the question frequently in your answer.
5. In every paragraph, make a **P**oint. **I**llustrate the point with *evidence* or *quotation*. **E**xplain the point. 

6. Arrange your creative, imaginative ideas in well-expressed, short paragraphs.
7. As you finish each paragraph, put your pen down and reread the question. Ask yourself: *Am I still answering the question I was asked?* Is there a further point to answer?
8. Finish with a strong sentence that reinforces the points you have made.
9. Pay careful attention to spelling and punctuation.

What features of quality does the examiner look for in a high scoring answer?

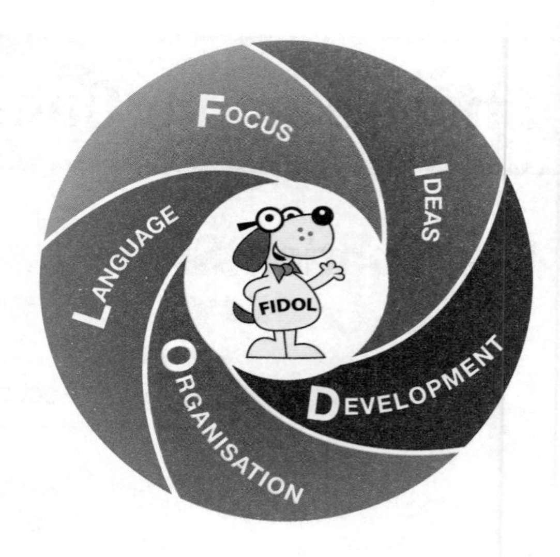

Focus
Ideas
Development = **FIDOL**
Organisation
Language

What does FIDOL mean?			
	I always do this	**I sometimes do this**	**I never do this**
Focus			
Answer the question you were asked			
Keep answering the question you were asked			
Use key words from the question in your answer			
Ideas			
Show that you have thought deeply about the question			
Make strong, relevant points			
Be imaginative and creative: write an answer that is a pleasure to read			
Development			
Make a statement, and then expand and explain that statement			
Back up what you say with accurate quotation or reference to detail in the text			
Organisation			
Divide your ideas into separate paragraphs, i.e. Introduction–Development–Conclusion			
Language			
Express yourself in good grammar			
Practise reading what you write aloud to test for mistakes, or awkward phrasing			
Use words that are appropriate for the situation: good vocabulary and correct English strengthen your points			
Show knowledge of and respect for correct spelling, and use punctuation marks where they are needed			

Tip

If you read a lot, you get better at writing interesting answers in good English.

How do I achieve organisation in my answers?

First, **read** the question carefully and **circle** the key words.

Do not rush into writing until you have grasped and noted the full demands of the question.

Remember!

If you answer only *part* of the question, you are marked out of *part* of the marks.

What should my answer look like on the page?

It should look like a series of ideas divided into a series of paragraphs.

How do I write a good opening paragraph?

Start with a short, clear opening sentence that responds directly to the question.

Briefly develop that sentence, weaving in the key words of the question.

Tell the examiner that **you intend to tackle each part of the question**.

As you practise writing answers in this section of the book:

Put your pen down after your first paragraph, and read it aloud.

Does it sound strong and clear?

Have you told the examiner that you will focus on the question that is being asked? ✔

Second paragraph – the development

Start with a **leader sentence**. A good example of this can be found on page 4 ('Mushrooms').

Develop, illustrate and explain your point, using evidence and/or quotation from the text or image.

When you put the full stop at the end, read over the paragraph and ask yourself the following questions:

Has the paragraph made one or two clear points?

Are the points illustrated?

Does it answer the question that was asked? ✔

Any further paragraphs should also begin with a **leader sentence**, as each paragraph is giving a new idea linked to the question. Keep **illustrating** and **explaining** your points.

Final paragraph

Bring the answer to a logical conclusion, summarising and reinforcing the points you have made.

Before you write your final paragraph:

Reread paragraphs 1 and 2, and with them in mind, sum it all up.

Your last sentence should be strong and clear. It's the last thing the examiner reads before giving your mark. ✔

So how will I learn all these skills? ✔

Practise **FIDOL** (**F**ocus **I**deas **D**evelopment **O**rganisation **L**anguage) in the following question on a film poster. ✔

Appreciating Visual Genres – The Film Poster

The examination question:

Write a critical analysis of the poster below for the film *The Glass Castle*.

In it, you should consider

- The visual impact of the poster

and

- Whether or not the poster makes you want to see the film.

The answer:

The examiner uses the following guidelines in marking your answer:

- The answer should analyse a number of aspects of the poster for the film.
- It should deal with each of the two bullet points in the question, but not necessarily equally depending on the marks given.
- Points made should be developed and illustrated with evidence and specific reference to the photograph.
- You may choose to want or not want to see the film.

To help you to write a good answer, here are some possible points:

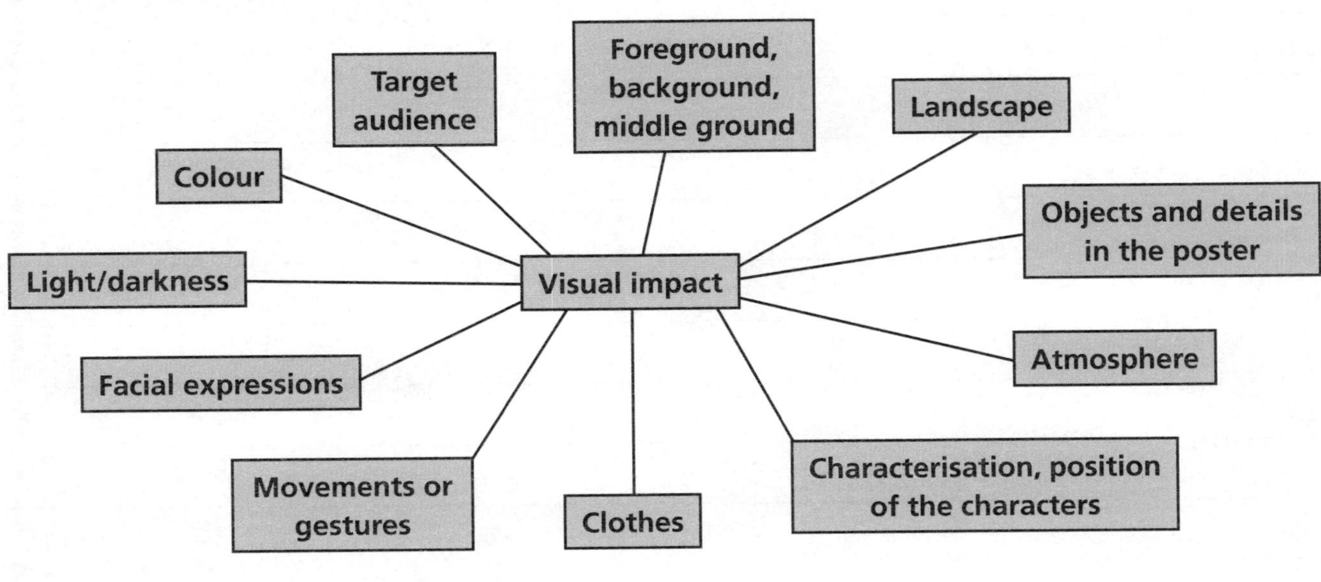

Whether the poster makes you want to see the film:

- I like ☐ don't like ☐ the content.
- The imagery is ☐ is not ☐ enticing or interesting.
- The poster does ☐ does not ☐ create a sense of the story.
- The characters appeal ☐ don't appeal ☐ to me.
- I like ☐ don't like ☐ the setting or the kind of story suggested.

Rough Work

The examination paper gives extra pages of writing space if needed. However, it is a good idea at this preparation stage to practise presenting your points in a series of quality paragraphs. You won't have the time or the space to write lots of unnecessary stuff in the exam!

The marking

When you have finished writing, read your answer aloud as if you were the examiner, using the following FIDOL-based questions.

F Did I answer the question I was asked? Did I use key words from the question in my answer?

I Does my answer show deep thought? Does it make strong, relevant, interesting points? Is it a pleasure to read my ideas?

D Did I develop, expand and explain my points? Did I back up points with accurate quotation or reference to the poster? Is my answer grounded in details from the poster?

O Are my ideas divided into separate paragraphs, with clear introduction, development and conclusion?

L Does my answer display good vocabulary and grammar, clear expression, and accurate spelling and punctuation? Have I learned the correct terms for analysing a visual text?

Place your answer in the high, medium or low score range, depending on your answers to the questions on the previous page.

	High (10–9)	**Medium (8–5)**	**Low (4–0)**	**If your answer is not in the high score range, what could you do to improve?**
Focus				
Ideas				
Development				
Organisation				
Language (Spelling & Punctuation)				

Responding to Spoken Texts – Appreciating Language, Register And Audience

People speak English differently according to the situation and the audience. The texts and assignments that follow will prepare you for examination questions that measure your ability to appreciate and describe the many different ways in which English is spoken. This is called **register**.

The **Oral Language**, **Reading** and **Writing** Learning Outcomes that are specified for the final examination state:

Students should be able to:

(OL) *Demonstrate how register, including grammar, text structure and word choice, varies with context and purpose in spoken texts.*

(R) *Read their texts to understand and appreciate language enrichment by examining an author's choice of words, the use and effect of simple figurative language, vocabulary and language patterns, and images, as appropriate to the text.*

(W) *Demonstrate an understanding of how syntax, grammar, text structure and word choice may vary with context and purpose.*

(Final Examination Requirements: English Specification, 13–15)

Sample 1

Read this extract from an after-match interview with a GAA manager.

Interviewer: Were you pleased with today's performance?

Manager: Yeah … well look … satisfied, relieved … We knew they were goin' to come at us … the lads worked their socks off … dug it out in the first half … took two sucker punches but knuckled down, staying bang on the game plan … there's backbone in these guys … nothing rocked us, we didn't flinch … goalkeeper delivered some laser-like kicks beyond mid-field … When PJ slapped it over the bar we knew we had it.

In fairness to the opposition, they kept knocking at the door, never let up … crowd got their money's worth … commitment, determination … brilliant day for the club, the families, boyfriends, girlfriends and fans.

Going forward, we'll take it one match at a time and we ain't goin' to flinch too handy.

What elements of the manager's response make it engaging for listeners?

In your answer, you should make reference to purpose, language, audience and impact in four separate paragraphs.

When you write your answer, underline the first sentence in each of your paragraphs. This will train you to make the **P**oint, and **I**llustrate and **E**xplain your point in each paragraph.

Remember!

Write a short, clear opening sentence that states your case. Then write a series of short paragraphs. Each paragraph has a separate point, stated, illustrated and explained.

Rough Work

When you have finished, read your answer aloud. Think of yourself as an examiner and place your answer in one of the three score ranges – **high**, **medium** or **low**.

Explain why you placed your answer in that category.

For example:

I placed my answer in the high score range for the following reasons. I started with a strong, clear sentence that clearly stated my case. I divided my answer into four paragraphs, each with a separate point. I started each paragraph with a strong, clear statement. I made good points and presented good ideas that were relevant to the question. I dealt with each key word in the question. I used quotations to illustrate my points. I explained my points clearly. I ended with a strong, clear sentence.

Sample 2

Read this famous sentence from President John F. Kennedy's 1961 inauguration speech.

> Ask not what your country can do for you – ask what you can do for your country.

Analyse the statement using the following headings: purpose, language, style, message, tone and impact.

Tip

Notice the use of:

- Simple one-syllable words
- Solemn language
- Contrast (negative and positive)
- Internal rhyme
- Splitting of sentence into halves

Rough Work

When you have finished writing:

- Reread pages 24–26 on FIDOL and organisation.
- Read over your answer as if you were the examiner.
- Fill in the grid below, putting your answer in one of the following categories in each of the FIDOL headings:

	High (10–9)	**Medium (8–5)**	**Low (4–0)**	**If your answer is not in the high score range, what could you do to improve?**
Focus				
Ideas				
Development				
Organisation				
Language (Spelling & Punctuation)				

Sample 3

Read the following extract from General Eisenhower's World War II speech, which was broadcast in June 1944 to 150,000 troops about to face the enemy on the Normandy beaches. Their mission was to liberate Europe from Nazi control.

Soldiers, sailors and airmen ...

You are about to embark upon the Great Crusade, toward which we have striven these many months. The eyes of the world are upon you. The hopes and prayers of liberty-loving people everywhere march with you. In company with our brave Allies and brothers-in-arms on other Fronts, you will bring about the destruction of the German war machine, the elimination of Nazi tyranny over the oppressed peoples of Europe, and security for ourselves in a free world.

Your task will not be an easy one. Your enemy is well trained, well equipped and battle-hardened. He will fight savagely.

Our Home Fronts have given us an overwhelming superiority in weapons and munitions of war, and placed at our disposal great reserves of trained fighting men.

The tide has turned! The free men of the world are marching together to Victory!

I have full confidence in your courage and devotion to duty and skill in battle. We will accept nothing less than full Victory!

In this speech, explain how the speaker shows understanding of his audience and uses language that suits his purpose.

Remember!

The examiner will expect your answer to deal with both aspects of this question. Remember to circle the key words or phrases and mention each of them in your answer.

Rough Work

Reading to Analyse and Evaluate

Students should be able to:

Listen actively in order to ... evaluate effectiveness of, and respond to ... media broadcasts ... noting key ideas, style ... and overall impact.

Identify and comment on features of English at word and sentence level using appropriate terminology, showing how such features contribute to overall effect.

(Final Examination Requirements: English Specification, 13–14)

The following promotional press release is taken from the RTÉ Press Centre. It announces a special documentary, *Pull Like a Dog*, on the O'Donovan brothers, Olympic medallists and champion rowers.

Explain what aspects of this press release would attract listeners to the documentary. Refer to aspects of the text to support your response.

Tip

Quote carefully chosen words, and make reference to lively images, use of humour and catchphrases.

27 December, 9:30pm, RTÉ One: ***Pull Like a Dog****, a special one-hour documentary follows the O'Donovan brothers as they return to their parish of Lisheen and Skibbereen rowing club in the aftermath of their success.*

In August 2016, Gary and Paul O'Donovan, two young rowers from West Cork, came from nowhere to become household names after bolting their way to silver medal success at the Rio Olympics. Not only did they become the first ever Irish rowers to bring home Olympic medals, but within a week Paul also went on to become the fastest singles lightweight rower on the planet by winning gold at the World Championships. With catchphrases like 'Pull like a dog' and 'Steak and spuds', these two young men have succeeded in warming the hearts of a nation.

This special one-hour documentary follows the O'Donovan brothers as they return to their parish of Lisheen and Skibbereen. We spend time in their home, on the beautiful river Ilen and inside their small club, which this year became the most successful club in Irish rowing history.

(presspack.rte.ie)

Rough Work

Reading for Comparison

Comparing the final words in films

Students should be able to:

Read for a variety of purposes: ... pleasure ... comparison.

(Final Examination Requirements: English Specification, 14)

The final words in a film may have a strong impact. These words give the audience something to remember about the character and/or about the story that has been told. They may reinforce the personality of the character and plant the seeds of a continuing story after the film has ended.

a. Read the final words spoken by the serial killer Hannibal Lecter in the film ***The Silence of the Lambs***. Hannibal, having just escaped from prison, telephones an FBI agent to tell her what he is about to do.

> I do wish we could chat longer, but ... I'm having an old friend for dinner. Bye.

b. Read Obi-Wan's final statement to Darth Vader in the closing moment of ***Star Wars Episode IV: A New Hope***.

> If you strike me down, I shall become more powerful than you can possibly imagine.

Choose the ending you think would have the greater impact on a cinema audience and give reasons for your choice.

Remember!

The examiner will be looking for:

- Clear focus on the question
- Creative and original ideas that show the candidate has thought deeply
- Development of the ideas with quotes and/or evidence
- A well-organised answer
- Good expression, spelling and punctuation

Rough Work

A quick reminder about the quality of examination answering:

An excellent answer will:	**A poor quality answer may:**
• Focus clearly on the question and keep that focus through every paragraph. • Present ideas that are original, thoughtful and relevant. • Show deep thought, originality and creativity, where appropriate. • Develop ideas. • Use accurate quotation and reference to details in the text to back up the points made. • Be well-organised and structured into separate paragraphs. • Use correct written English. • Show good expression, good grammar and an extensive vocabulary. • Spell and use punctuation very accurately.	• Lack focus on the task and struggle to address the question. • Show a lack of understanding of the task set in the question. • Answer only one part of the question. • Begin well, but lose focus and go off the point. • Summarise rather than analyse. • Present ideas that are unclear or irrelevant, showing little deep thought. • State ideas, but leave them undeveloped. • Neglect to use reference or quotation. • Quote inaccurately or carelessly. • Be poorly paragraphed and disorganised. • Be poorly expressed. • Spell and use punctuation poorly.

Comparing novel openings – Appreciating setting and storytelling

Funeral Voices

When the doorbell rings at three in the morning, it's never good news.

Alex Rider was woken by the first chime. His eyes flickered open, but for a moment he stayed completely still in his bed, lying on his back with his head resting on the pillow. He heard a bedroom door open and a creak of wood as somebody went downstairs. The bell rang a second time, and he looked at the alarm clock glowing beside him. There was a rattle as someone slid the security chain off the front door.

Anthony Horowitz, ***Stormbreaker***

The Los Angeles Institute, December 2007

On the day Emma Carstair's parents were killed, the weather was perfect.

On the other hand, the weather was usually perfect in Los Angeles. Emma's mother and father dropped her off on a clear winter morning at the Institute in the hills behind the Pacific Coast Highway overlooking the blue ocean. The sky was a cloudless expanse that stretched from the cliffs of the Pacific Palisades to the beaches at Point Dume.

Cassandra Clare, ***City of Heavenly Fire***

Compare and contrast.

This means you must find something similar **and** something different!

- Identify **one technique** that is used by **both** writers to try to 'hook' the reader.
- Point out one **different** technique used by one of the writers to capture the reader's attention and create interest in the story.

Remember!

A good novelist 'hooks' the reader with his or her opening paragraph. Novelists use many different techniques to engage the reader's imagination **and** create interest in the story that is to be told.

How to answer 'compare and contrast' questions:

The examiner will expect an answer to deal with each part of the question.

The answer should both compare and contrast, i.e. point out similarities and differences. Identify one technique that the two paragraphs have in common.

Then point out how the paragraphs are different or contrasting.

Possible points you could make include:

- Interesting opening sentence
- Naming the central character
- Character has suffered sadness or loss
- Dramatic death or crime
- Use of imagery (sight and sound)
- Creating an interesting scene
- Good descriptive writing
- Beautiful setting
- Suspense
- Atmosphere
- Interesting or appealing words and phrases

Rough Work

Responding to Texts – Appreciating Language, Story and Action

Students should be able to:

Read their texts for understanding and appreciation of character, setting, story and action.

Write for a variety of purposes … to … engage … inform … persuade … comment on what they have … read.

(Final Examination Requirements: English Specification, 14–15)

Alexandria 125 BC

The assassins dropped into the palace grounds at midnight, four fleet shadows dark against the wall. The fall was high, the ground was hard; they made no more sound on impact than the pattering of rain. Three seconds they crouched there, low and motionless, sniffing at the air. Then away they stole, through the dark gardens, among the tamarisks and date palms, towards the quarters when the boy lay at rest, a cheetah on a chain stirred in its sleep; far away in the desert, jackals cried.

They went on pointed toe-tips, leaving no trace in the long wet grass. Their robes flittered at their backs, fragmenting their shadows into wisps and traces. What could be seen? Nothing but leaves shifting in the breeze. What could be heard? Nothing but the wind sighing among the palm fronds. No sight, no noise. A crocodile djinni,* standing sentry at the sacred pool, was undisturbed though they passed within a scale's breadth of his tail. For humans, it wasn't badly done.

The heat of the day was a memory; the air was chill. Above the palace a cold round moon shone down, slathering silver across the roofs and courtyards.

At their posts, the guards played games of chance. In the pillared halls, the servants slept on beds of rushes. The palace gates were locked by triple bolts, each thicker than a man. No eyes were turned to the western gardens, where death came calling, secret as a scorpion, on four pairs of silent feet.

The boy's window was on the first floor of the palace. Four black shadows hunched beneath the wall. The leader made a signal. One by one they pressed against the stonework; one by one they began to climb, suspended by their fingertips and the nails of their big toes.

Jonathan Stroud, ***Ptolemy's Gate***

*A supernatural spirit which can take human or animal form.

A. In the opening paragraph on the previous page, point out:

1. Two examples of alliteration

___

___

2. Three examples of a good choice of verb

___

___

___

3. The noun that tells you a murder is planned

___

4. Two examples of sound images

___

___

5. One example of a dramatic visual image

___

___

6. Two details that give you a strong sense of the setting

___

___

B. In the space below, explain in your own words what is happening in this opening scene.

C. Write a promotional press release for this novel, telling readers that the first page will grip them. Base your writing only on the extract above.

Rough Work

Responding to the Special Language of Poetry

Mushrooms

Overnight, very
Whitely, discreetly,
Very quietly

Our toes, our noses
Take hold on the loam,
Acquire the air.

Nobody sees us,
Stops us, betrays us;
The small grains make room.

Soft fists insist on
Heaving the needles,
The leafy bedding,

Even the paving.
Our hammers, our rams,
Earless and eyeless,

Perfectly voiceless,
Widen the crannies,
Shoulder through holes. We

Diet on water,
On crumbs of shadow,
Bland-mannered, asking

Little or nothing.
So many of us!
So many of us!

We are shelves, we are
Tables, we are meek,
We are edible,

Nudgers and shovers
In spite of ourselves.
Our kind multiplies:

We shall by morning
Inherit the earth.
Our foot's in the door.

Sylvia Plath

The title of the poem is 'Mushrooms'. In your opinion, does it simply describe mushrooms, or might it tell another story? Write your interpretation of the poem, justifying your opinion with quotation from the text.

Remember!

- Make a **P**oint
- **I**llustrate the point with a quotation
- **E**xplain your point

Rough Work

Reading Comprehension Strategies

Students should be able to:

Identify [and] appreciate ... the ways in which different ... digital and visual genres ... shape texts and shape the reader's experience of them.

(Final Examination Requirement: English Specification, 14)

Study the homepage of NASA, the National Aeronautics and Space Administration, below. NASA's mission is 'to pioneer the future in space exploration, scientific discovery and aeronautics research'.

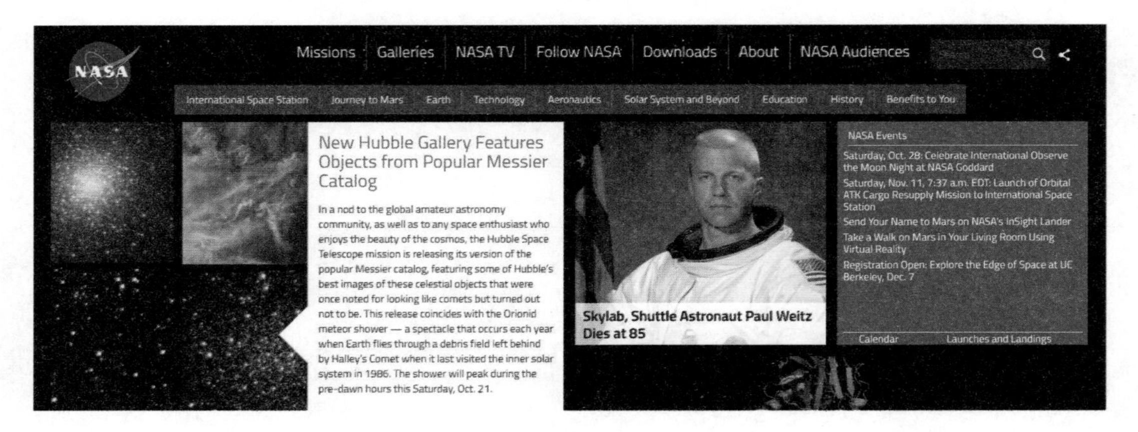

Imagine that you are presenting this website page to your teachers and Student Council who are designing a website to promote your school to potential parents and students.

Write a talk in which you have the page up on screen and you are commenting on it.

In your talk, point out the elements on the page that you consider to be informative, carefully arranged, and/or appealing. Explain how these elements could become part of your school website's homepage.

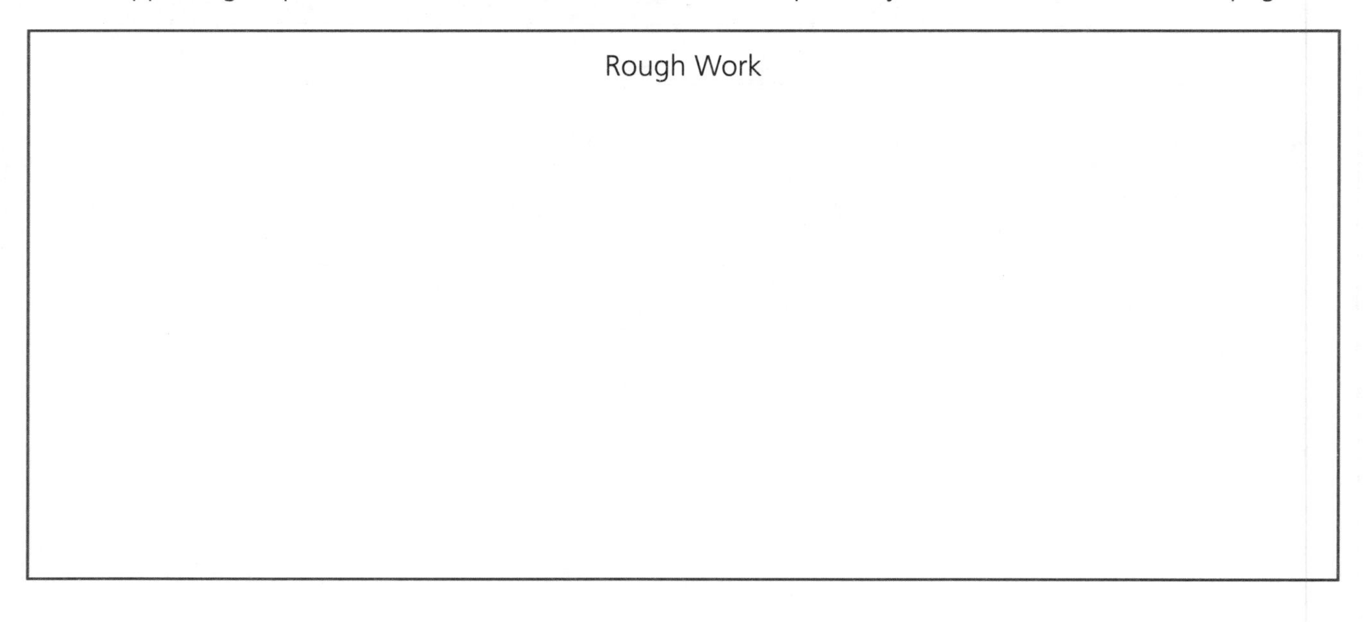

Responding to Shakespeare

Introduction

Shakespeare's plays are divided into five **acts**. Each act is divided into **scenes**. They are written in **blank verse**, i.e. **unrhymed iambic pentameter**. This means that each line can be broken down into ten **syllables** (or beats) composed in pairs of a weak beat followed by a heavy beat. In some plays, before the story starts, there is a **prologue** spoken in rhyme by a chorus or single actor. Occasionally, the play ends with an **epilogue**, i.e. a short **afterword** that 'rounds off' the play, perhaps adding a witty or profound comment on theme, story or character.

The correct term for conversation in a play is **dialogue**. An **aside** is a line spoken to the audience that cannot be heard by the other characters. **Exit** means a single character leaves the stage; **exeunt** means more than one character leaves the stage.

The plots present characters in **conflict**. A character may struggle with other people, with society's rules or with him/herself; his/her own feelings, morality, ambition, etc. The turning point of the action and moment of greatest tension is called the **climax**. When the tension is released and the **conflict** has been resolved, we see the **falling action** of the play.

When a Shakespearean character speaks lines which are understood in a double sense by the audience, but not by the character, this is called **verbal irony**. When events turn out in a way that is the very opposite of what might have been expected, this is called **dramatic irony**.

At moments of great emotion, a character may speak his or her deepest thoughts and feelings in a **soliloquy**, a speech heard by the audience but not by other characters on the stage. Some of Shakespeare's plays have a **sub-plot**, a small story with minor characters that runs parallel to the greater, main plot.

The **theme** is the central concern or idea that unifies the entire play.

Shakespeare's plays can be divided into **comedies**, **tragedies** and **histories**.

Staging

Practise taking a key scene and imagining how it could be creatively staged. Use the correct terms – upstage (at the back), downstage (at the front), stage left and stage right.

... look

Who are the characters on the stage?

Where are they positioned?

Setting: backdrop, furniture, props

Lighting: where the stage should be bright and where dark

Colours

Costumes, jewellery, hairstyles, etc.

... sound

Tone of voice in dialogue and speeches

Music – if any: What kind of music, played by what instrument(s) would suit the action?

Should the music be soft or loud?

Sound effects: Go to your key scenes and see where you might have sounds such as swords clashing, drumbeats, sound of weeping, shouts, cheers, howling wind, birdsong or cries, waves crashing, etc. Use your imagination as you visualise the scene!

Hamlet

Father and son

In this scene, Polonius is saying goodbye to his son, Laertes, who is travelling from his home in Denmark to study at university in France. Polonius says he should hurry on board because the wind is right for sailing and he's delaying the ship. But he can't let him go without giving him some fatherly advice, so he makes a long speech. He tells him to pay attention to some advice about when to talk and when to be silent; when to take someone on; how to dress and look after his public image; and what he should do regarding money.

Polonius:

Yet here, Laertes! Aboard, aboard, for shame!
The wind sits in the shoulder of your sail,
And you are stay'd for. There; my blessing with thee!
And these few precepts in thy memory
See thou character. Give thy thoughts no tongue,
Nor any unproportion'd thought his act.
Be thou familiar, but by no means vulgar.
Those friends thou hast, and their adoption tried,
Grapple them to thy soul with hoops of steel;
But do not dull thy palm with entertainment
Of each new-hatch'd, unfledg'd* comrade. Beware
Of entrance to a quarrel but, being in,
Bear't that th' opposed may beware of thee.
Give every man thy ear, but few thy voice;
Take each man's censure,** but reserve thy judgement.
Costly thy habit as thy purse can buy,
But not express'd in fancy; rich, not gaudy;
For the apparel oft proclaims the man;
And they in France of the best rank and station
Are of a most select and generous chief in that.
Neither a borrower nor a lender be;
For loan oft loses both itself and friend,
And borrowing dulls the edge of husbandry.***
This above all: to thine own self be true,
And it must follow, as the night the day,
Thou canst not then be false to any man.

*newborn, too young to have feathers

**criticism

***managing money

A. There are **10** questions to be answered.

Score **2** marks for each correct answer. **20** gives you full marks.

1. Write the lines that are closest in meaning to:

   Remember these few things I am telling you

   ____

   ____

2. Which of the following is the best rewording of the lines:

   Give thy thoughts no tongue,
   Nor any unproportion'd thought his act.

   A. Don't think badly about people
   B. Do something as soon as a thought strikes you
   C. Keep your opinions to yourself and don't rush into action before thinking things through

   ☐

3. Which line is closest in meaning to the phrase:

   Don't say aloud what you are thinking in your head

   ____

4. Which line is closest in meaning to the phrase:

   Do more listening than talking

   ____

5. Which adjectives best describe the behaviour that Polonius has advised as far as line 7:
   A. Be reserved, discreet, loyal and respected
   B. Be shrewd and generous
   C. Be outspoken and very friendly

   ☐

6. Which of the following is the best rewording of the lines:

   Costly thy habit as thy purse can buy,
   But not express'd in fancy; rich, not gaudy

   A. Buy very expensive purses
   B. Make a lot of money
   C. Buy the best clothes you can afford, but never look overdressed

   ☐

7. Which word best describes Polonius as he speaks to his son?
   A. Aggressive
   B. Cautious
   C. Irritated

   ☐

8. Which of these statements is true?
   A. Polonius believes clothes are unimportant
   B. Polonius believes your clothes should be very striking and ostentatious
   C. Polonius believes you should buy the best clothes you can afford

9. Which of these statement is true?
   A. Polonius believes that French people are arrogant
   B. Polonius admires French taste in clothes
   C. Polonius thinks the French spend too much

10. Write the lines that are closest in meaning to:

    You will lose not only your friend, but your money too

    ____

    ____

My score out of **20** is _____.

B. This is a very long speech. Explain **two** imaginative things a director could do to stage this long speech from the play.

Tip

The examiner will be looking for your knowledge of **stagecraft** and will expect you to pay attention to the word '**imaginative**'. Your ideas should relate to detail in the speech and show creativity and imagination.

Rough Work

Richard III

The soliloquy on the next page is the opening speech in Shakespeare's play *Richard III*.

I will be king! I'll murder anyone who stands in my way, starting with my brother Clarence!

The opening scene in a modern performance of *Richard III*

As the play begins, Edward, King of England, is dying.

A terrible civil war has just ended. The peaceful country is now bright and happy. War-weary soldiers are looking for romance. Richard feels left out of all this happiness. He says there is no point in looking for love, because he is ugly. Instead, he will look for power. He plans to turn the king against his older brother, Clarence (the heir to the throne), and put him in prison. Then Richard will arrange to have Clarence murdered.

Richard alone on stage:

Now is the winter of our discontent
Made glorious summer by this sun of York;
And all the clouds that lour'd upon our house
In the deep bosom of the ocean buried.
Now are our brows bound with victorious wreaths,
Our bruisèd arms hung up for monuments;
Grim-visag'd war hath smooth'd his wrinkled front;
Our stern alarums changed to merry meetings,
Our dreadful marches to delightful measures.
And now, instead of mounting barbed steeds
To fright the souls of fearful adversaries,
He capers nimbly in a lady's chamber
To the lascivious pleasing of a lute.
But I, that am not shap'd for sportive tricks,
Nor made to court an amorous looking-glass;
Deform'd, unfinish'd, sent before my time
Into this breathing world scarce half made up,
And that so lamely and unfashionable
That dogs bark at me as I halt by them;
And therefore, since I cannot prove a lover,
To entertain these fair well-spoken days,
I am determined to prove a villain,
And hate the idle pleasures of these days.
Plots have I laid, libels, and dreams,
To set my brother Clarence and the king
In deadly hate the one against the other:
And if King Edward be as true and just
As I am subtle, false and treacherous,
This day should Clarence closely be mew'd up,
About a prophecy, which says that 'G'
Of Edward's heirs the murderer shall be.
Dive, thoughts, down to my soul: here
Clarence comes.

Mini glossary

sun of York – King Edward, whose family name was York

stern alarums – battlefield bugles

delightful measures – dance steps

court an amorous looking-glass – admire myself in a mirror

subtle – sly, cunning

mew'd up – locked up in prison

'G' … the murderer shall be – Richard was Duke of **G**loucester

1. Match the character to the description.
   A. Richard
   B. Edward
   C. Clarence

The character who is speaking the soliloquy	
Richard's older brother, who is in line to become king on the death of the present king	
The King of England as the play begins	

2. Write the words from the speech that match the modern English versions below.

Our dark, unhappy time has been changed to sunshine days	
Dark-faced war	
Instead of climbing on to armed horses	
To frighten terrifying enemies	
A word that means *smartly, quickly*	
A woman's bedroom	
I was not created athletic and sporty	
Ugly, badly made, premature and small when I was born into this world	
I have decided to be evil	
Time to hide what I'm thinking; here comes Clarence	

3. If you were the actor playing Richard on stage, explain how you would keep the audience interested throughout this long opening speech. In your answer, you may refer to your voice, your gestures, props, where you would stand, sit or walk, etc.

Tip

Imagine how the speech should be spoken to make it sound **dramatic**. Vary your **volume**, **tone** and **facial expressions**. Add some dramatic **gestures** to keep the audience watching and listening as you speak. **Pause** occasionally to give them time to take it all in. Mention any **props** that you think would help to act out the speech. Explain the **emotions** that you would show.

An example of rough work has been done for you to give you some ideas.

Rough Work

Richard centre stage ... walk slowly downstage, head held high, make eye contact with the audience ... not speak for a few moments for dramatic effect ... bend forward ... look directly at the people in the front row

Needs a walking stick to lean on.

Army costume? General with big, fancy gold epaulettes, braid ... the emotions I see here are pride and arrogance and even madness ... proud, arrogant, self-centred show-off ... war medals – speak some lines loudly, triumphantly, whisper some lines with an evil, sarcastic grin ... Look around slyly to check no one is listening

When I describe my deformed body, suddenly change smiling face to a sneer – spit out the lines viciously and savagely ... sad, lonely man ... no loving relationships ...

'I am determined to prove a villain' in a snarling whisper that sounds like a horrible threat.

I imagine hearing warlike music and the loud banging of drums and the beating of his walking stick on the wooden floorboards in time with the music.

The setting is bare and dark ... black background hints that there are dark, evil happenings going on behind the scenes ...

I would hold their attention by shocking them, telling them that I hate my ugly face and body and I have evil plans. I will kill my own brother. If I can't be loved, then I will be feared.

... Laugh hysterically, as if mad ... stop when I hear footsteps from the side stage ...

At the end of the speech, put finger to lips, look around to check that no one can hear, grin ... 'sshh' ... turn and run to the back of the stage, smiling slyly, big, false smile to welcome Clarence as if delighted to see him.

Your Studied Shakespeare Play

Having answered on an unseen extract, you may then be asked to write about your studied play. To prepare for this studied part of the question, you can fill in the templates below.

Carefully write the name of the play you studied, using capital letters where needed, spelling each word correctly and placing inverted commas at the beginning and end.

Fill in the gaps below for practice:

___*omeo and* ___*uliet*

___*he* ___*erchant of* ___*enice*

___*ulius* ___*aesar*

Remember!

You make a bad impression if you spell 'Shakespeare' incorrectly. You ***Shake*** the ***spear*** and add '**e**'.

Your studied play

Complete the paragraph below, giving careful attention to spelling and capital letters.

The Shakespearean play I studied is ______________________________.

It is set in ______________________________.

The **major** characters are ______________________________

______________________________.

The **minor** characters are ______________________________

______________________________.

It is worthwhile to make a special study of the opening scene of your studied Shakespeare. In these opening moments, Shakespeare sets the scene for his story, introduces characters and often introduces the theme of the play. Read carefully, imagine the staging and be able to write in detail about the opening as your first key moment.

Here is a description of the **opening scene** from my studied Shakespeare play.

Characters on stage:

___

___

The setting is:

___

___

This is what happens:

___

___

___

Here are two quotations from the scene:

___

___

Here are my ideas for this **opening scene** as performed on stage.

Backdrop:

___

___

At **stage right** you would see:

___

At **stage left** you would see:

___

Upstage you would see:

___

Downstage you would see:

___

Lighting:

Costumes:

Position of characters:

Their gestures and/or **movements**:

Music and sound effects:

What else?

Remember!

A **key moment** (or scene) is one in which we experience great emotional intensity or understanding of theme, character or motivation. It is a special moment that stays in our memory because it is so packed with meaning. We recognise its importance to the plot or to our understanding of the characters, their society or their story.

Here is another **key scene** from the play that I know very well and am able to quote from.

Act ___ Scene ___

Characters on stage:

____

____

This is what happens:

____

____

____

____

It's a key scene because:

____

____

____

____

Here are three quotations from the scene:

____

____

____

Here are my ideas for **this key scene** performed on stage.

Backdrop:

____

____

At **stage right** you would see:

____

At **stage left** you would see:

____

Upstage you would see:

____

Downstage you would see:

____

Lighting:

Costumes:

Position of characters:

Their gestures and/or **movements**:

Music and sound effects:

What else?

Here is a description one further key moment, which may be taken from the **closing scene**.

Characters on stage:

____

____

The setting is:

____

____

This is what happens:

____

____

____

Here are two quotations from the scene:

____

____

Here are my ideas for this **closing scene** as performed on stage.

Backdrop:

____

____

At **stage right** you would see:

____

At **stage left** you would see:

____

Upstage you would see:

____

Downstage you would see:

____

Lighting:

____

____

Costumes:

Position of characters:

Their gestures and/or **movements**:

Music and sound effects:

What else?

Write about Your Studied Texts

Students should be able to:

Respond imaginatively in writing to their texts showing a critical appreciation of language, style and content, choice of words, language patterns, tone, images.

(Final Examination Requirement: English Specification, 15)

Novels and Short Stories

Page to screen

Write a pitch to a film producer, persuading this person that a **novel** or **short story** that you have studied on your course has the potential to become a great film.

EXAMPLE: *Jane Eyre*

Here are words and phrases you could use in a four-paragraph answer.

1. Storyline/plot

great plot with many twists and turns
misery to happiness   love story   humiliation
brutal boarding school   hunger and cold   loneliness
mystery   dark secret   romance   forgiveness
fairytale ending

2. Characters

orphaned heroine   poor relation
horrible aunt and cousins   cruel schoolmaster
kind teacher   gentle, delicate friend
spoiled, selfish young man squanders family fortune
great names: Brocklehurst, Grace Poole, Rochester
handsome hero with secret past
mad woman in the attic

3. Dramatic moments

red room   fire in bedroom
Rochester's first appearance
ruined wedding ceremony
fire in big house
Jane's vision

4. Screen potential

potential for emotional musical score
variety of costumes   cinematic settings   carriages   window seats   dark, creepy interiors   oil lamps   stormy skies
countryside   burning mansion

Now it's your turn ...

Short story or novel	Author

Make four word clouds with words and phrases you will use under these four headings:

Storyline/plot **Characters** **Dramatic moments** **Screen potential**

Each heading will become a paragraph in your answer.

Write your four-paragraph pitch, beginning:

I believe that ______________________________ has the potential to become a great film because ...

Remember!

Make sure that you can spell titles and names correctly, and that you check your spelling in the exam.

Rough Work

Interview

1. Think of a well-known television interviewer. Compose a list of questions that this person might ask in an interview with a character (major or minor) in one of your studied novels.

   A. ______

   B. ______

   C. ______

   D. ______

   E. ______

2. Working with a partner, rehearse the interview, deciding on the answers the character might give. Then present your interview to your classmates.

Endings

Compare the endings of two short stories you have read.

In the boxes below give the titles and authors of TWO of the short stories you have studied on your course. Marks are awarded for giving full titles and names with correct spelling.

EXAMPLE

First story	Second story
Title: 'Guests of the Nation'	Title: 'The Landlady'
Author: Frank O'Connor	Author: Roald Dahl

Rough Work

	First ending	Second ending
Who are the characters?	An elderly woman who was sheltering IRA men; Noble, a young IRA man; Bonaparte, the narrator of the story, who thought guarding the prisoners was not very serious and who never saw them as hostages.	An eccentric and very strange elderly landlady of a bed and breakfast; 17-year-old Billy Weaver, a very naïve, innocent young man on his first time away from home.
What is happening?	Two prisoners who had been held hostage have just been shot. The narrator is standing at the door of the cottage, shocked by what has happened, looking out at the bogland and up at the stars. Noble and the old woman are praying, he by the fire, she in the doorway. The narrator has pushed past them to stand looking out at the bog.	Billy is drinking strange-tasting tea. The landlady is asking him if he has signed the book so that she can look it up later on. She holds up her teacup, and smiling, tells him that he is the only guest in the past three years.
Where and when is the ending set?	On a dark winter's evening. An old cottage in a remote bogland somewhere in Ireland. Pitch black darkness lit only by the stars in the night sky. Silence broken by birds shrieking.	On a dark winter's evening in the town of Bath, in the sitting room of an old, neglected house, full of stuffed animals.
Quote a memorable phrase or sentence.	Anything that happened to me afterwards, I never felt the same about again.	'No, my dear,' she said. 'Only you.'

	First ending (cont.)	Second ending (cont.)
What words or phrase would you use to describe the ending?	The words that best describe this ending are sad, terrifying, shocking and full of deep emotion. Something terrible has happened that the narrator could never have imagined in his life before this happening. The ending is desolate, bewildered, painful and filled with grief.	This is a twist, which means an unexpected and very strange turn of events that takes the reader by surprise. In this case the twist is black humour, because it suggests that the tea is poisoned, and the innocent-seeming landlady is actually a murderer.
What are the characters' emotions?	The narrator is stunned, silent and fearful. His life has changed in that one night. He cannot speak because he is thinking about the grave of the two prisoners. He says he feels 'very small and very lost and lonely' but he really 'can't describe it'.	Billy is beginning to feel very suspicious and afraid of the situation he is in. The landlady seems pleased with the situation, as if all has gone to plan for her.

Now it's your turn ...

Name your chosen stories and their authors.

First story	Second story
Title:	Title:
Author:	Author:

Rough work

	First ending	Second ending
Who are the characters?		
What is happening?		

	First ending (cont.)	Second ending (cont.)
Where and when is the ending set?		
Quote a memorable phrase or sentence.		
What words or phrase would you use to describe the ending?		
What are the characters' emotions?		

Rough Work

Drama

Students should be able to:

Write about the effectiveness of key moments from their texts commenting on characters, key scenes, favourite images from a film … a drama.

(Final Examination Requirement: English Specification, 15)

Stagecraft in a key moment

Describe a stage performance of the opening scene of a play you have studied.

Your answer should include any or all of the following: characters, setting, sound effects, props, colours, lighting.

Rough Work

small village pub   south-west of Ireland   eldest son
small children playing pitch and toss   grumpy cattle dealer
prop: a sweeping brush   dim light   table   bar stools   rough-talking father
nervous son   bare brown walls   bare floorboards   old shabby clothes
dull colours   door to the side of stage

Here is a sample answer describing the opening scene from *The Field* by John B. Keane.

The opening scene of 'The Field' by John B. Keane is set in a dark, old-fashioned, rough bar in 'a small village in the south-west of Ireland'. The lighting is dim, the walls are brown and the only furniture is a few old wooden stools, a table and a wooden bar. A sweeping brush lies on the bare, dusty floorboards. A teenage boy is playing pitch and toss with younger children, who are hiding and laughing under a table. It begins with the slam of a door, stage right, and the sound of a strong wind when the narrow door opens and in comes a small, grumpy, thin man, Bird, rubbing his hands and stamping his feet on the floorboards, making a cloud of dust and dirt.

'Give us a half of whiskey for God's sake, Leamy.'

You can hear the happy giggling of toddlers until Leamy's father comes in and scatters the little children, who are afraid of him. I imagine all the characters wearing dull, old, shabby clothes. Then he turns on his son and snarls in a rough voice:

"Tis too fond you are of hanging about with women and children, 'Tis a daughter you should have been, not a son.'

Leamy looks put down by his father's insult but doesn't bite back, so maybe he is used to being spoken to like that. In a small voice, he says,

'Yes, Da.'

We suspect that this father bosses everyone around in his house. Although he has been told that his wife is feeding the baby, he says,

'Go and ask your mother will the dinner be ready soon.'

Now it's your turn ...

Describe a stage performance of a **key scene** of a play you have studied.

The characters on stage: men, women, names, ages, etc.	
Where are they positioned? What are they doing?	
Costumes and colours they are wearing – make-up, jewellery, hairstyles, etc.	
Can you see facial expressions? Describe their voices.	
Does the scene tell you anything about the story to come, or about relationships between people?	
What furniture/props can you see?	
What are the dominant colours/ lighting?	
Is there a backdrop? What does it show? Are there props?	
Any music or sound effects?	
Quote two lines from the scene.	

Rough Work

Stage to screen: Play to film

Write a pitch to a film producer, persuading him or her that a play that you have studied on your course has the potential to become a great film.

EXAMPLE: *Romeo and Juliet*

Add to the words and phrases in the word clouds below

Rough work

1. Storyline/plot

great plot unexpected twists and turns
family feud love story fight scenes
conflict swordplay

2. Characters

beautiful young heroine

3. Dramatic moments

first meeting fight scene
death of Tybalt

4. Screen potential

Now it's your turn ...

Name your studied drama (which may be *Romeo and Juliet*).

Play	Author

Make four word clouds with words and phrases you will use under these four headings:

Storyline/plot **Characters** **Dramatic moments** **Screen potential**

Each heading will become a paragraph in your answer.

Write your four-paragraph pitch, beginning:

I believe that ______________________________ has the potential to become a great film because ...

Rough Work

Promote the film with visual images

In the following boxes, describe two posters that would promote the film of the play you have chosen.

Poetry

Students should be able to:

Respond imaginatively in writing to their texts showing a critical appreciation of language, style and content, choice of words ... and images.

(Final Examination Requirement: English Specification, 15)

Compare TWO poems that gave you a strong sense of place. In your opinion, which poet creates the stronger sense of place? Give reasons for your choice, with detailed reference to both of your chosen poems.

EXAMPLE

First poem	**Second poem**
Title: 'The Lake Isle of Innisfree'	Title: 'The Listeners'
Author: W. B. Yeats	Author : Walter de la Mare

Complete the following table:

	First poem	**Second poem**
Where is the place described? Is it named?	The Lake Isle of Innisfree. A real island in Sligo	Deep in a forest
Who is speaking in the poem?	W. B. Yeats himself	An unnamed traveller on horseback
What can be seen in this place?	A small cabin, a beehive, waves, linnets, purple glow at noon	A lonely house, a turret, ferny floor, stars in the night sky, a bird, an empty hall, moonbeams, phantoms
What can be heard?	Waves lapping, bees buzzing, birds' wings flapping, sound of the cricket	Loud knocking on the door
When is the poem set? In history? In day or night?		
Do any poetic techniques help to give a strong sense of place?		
Quote your favourite phrase(s) or line(s) in the poem. Give reasons for your choices.		

In the sample answer below, the student has used:

- Words and phrases that **compare** and **contrast**.
- **Key words and phrases from the question**.
- The **correct vocabulary** words to write about a poem, rhythm, imagery, alliteration etc. These are all underlined throughout the answer, but you don't need to do this in the exam.

Sample answer:

'The Lake Isle of Innisfree' ('TLI of I') is a peaceful poem which describes a real island in Sligo. Yeats knew it and loved it from his holidays there as a child. In contrast, 'The Listeners' ('TL') is a dramatic poem describing an imaginary house in a moonlit forest which is visited by a mystery traveller on horseback. Both poems give me a strong sense of a very quiet place.

Yeats's beautiful island has a small cabin, and a beehive. He stands on the 'pavement grey' in London, hearing in his heart the buzzing of the bees and crickets, the flapping wings of the linnets and the waves lapping the Innisfree shore. In contrast, Walter de la Mare's sinister, scary house in the forest is full of strange ghosts. The scary sounds are the fluttering of bats, and the angry knocking on the door. The rhythm in each poem is slow, but in 'TLI of I' this rhythm is slow, relaxing and dreamy, whereas in 'TL' it is sinister and creates a mood of suspense.

Both poets create a strong sense of place. However, Yeats's poem simply describes, whereas Walter de la Mare tells a story. In my opinion, the sense of place is stronger in 'TL' for three reasons, i.e. the eerie atmosphere, the mystery story and the moonlit setting of the empty house, forest and phantoms.

The images of sight and sound in this poem give it the strongest sense of place in any poem I have studied. It starts with a dramatic sound and sight image, knocking on the moonlit door. I like the alliteration in 'the forest's ferny floor'. Then he looks up to the 'starred and leafy sky'. I can see it all like a scene in a film.

The best images creating suspense are 'moonbeams on the dark stair ... the empty hall'. My favourite line comes near the end. I like the alliteration in 'the silence surged softly backwards', as the horseman rides away. To the dramatic sound of 'plunging hoofs', the forest, the empty house and the ghosts fade away from our imaginations.

Here are some other poems that give a sense of place:

'Composed upon Westminster Bridge'	William Wordsworth
'Stopping by Woods on a Snowy Evening'	Robert Frost
'Back in the Playground Blues'	Adrian Mitchell
'Inniskeen Road: July Evening'	Patrick Kavanagh

Now it's your turn ...

Compare TWO poems that gave you a strong sense of place. One of the chosen poems may be 'The Lake Isle of Innisfree' OR 'The Listeners'. In your opinion, which poet creates the stronger sense of place? Give reasons for your choice, with detailed reference to both of your chosen poems.

Tip

Circle or underline the key words in the question before you start planning your answer.

First poem	Second poem
Title:	Title:
Author:	Author:

Plan your answer with rough notes.

	First poem	Second poem
Where is the place described? Is it named?		
Who is speaking in the poem?		
What can be seen in this place?		
What can be heard?		
When is the poem set? In history? In day or night?		
Do any poetic techniques help to give a strong sense of place?		
Quote your favourite phrase(s) or line(s) in the poem. Give reasons for your choices.		

Poems about people

Compare TWO poems that present a **person**. In your opinion, which poet creates the stronger sense of this person? Support the points you make with reference to both of your chosen poems.

Here is a selection of poems that present people:

'The New Boy'	John Walsh
'Little Red Riding Hood'	Roald Dahl
'Timothy Winters'	Charles Causley
'The Listeners'	Walter de la Mare
'When all the others were away at Mass', 'Mid-Term Break'	Seamus Heaney
'On Turning Ten'	Billy Collins
'The General', 'Base Details'	Siegfried Sassoon
'Memory of My Father'	Patrick Kavanagh
'She – Is Like a Bubble'	Elaine George
'Epitaph on a Tyrant'	W. H. Auden
'Shall I compare thee to a summer's day?'	William Shakespeare
'She Dwelt among the Untrodden Ways'	William Wordsworth
'Night Feed'	Eavan Boland

In the boxes below, give the titles and authors of TWO of the 'people' poems you have studied on your course.

First poem	**Second poem**
Title:	Title:
Author:	Author:

Remember!

- Use words and phrases that compare and contrast (i.e. similarities and differences).
- Use words and phrases from the question to keep you on task.
- Bring some poetic terms you know into your answer, e.g. imagery, metaphor, simile, alliteration, assonance, etc.
- Tell the examiner which is your favourite line and why you like it.

Plan your answer. Make rough notes to compare or contrast.

	First poem	Second poem
Where is the place described? Is it named?		
Who is speaking in the poem?		
What can be seen in this place?		
What can be heard?		
When is the poem set? In history? In day or night?		
Do any poetic techniques help to give a strong sense of place?		
Quote your favourite phrase(s) or line(s) in the poem. Give reasons for your choices.		

Tip

Use some of the following comparative phrases in your answer:

- Just as
- In contrast
- In much the same way
- However
- Likewise
- Unlike
- On the other hand
- On the contrary
- The opposite
- Compared to
- Equally
- As

Write your answer.

Film

Students should be able to:

Write about the effectiveness of key moments from their texts commenting on characters, key scenes, favourite images from a film.

(Final Examination Requirement: English Specification, 15)

1. In the boxes provided below, name the film you studied for this course and give the name of the film's director.

Film title:
Director:

2. Describe the **setting** of the film you studied using the three following headings to guide your response: (i) location, (ii) mood/atmosphere, (iii) social values.

3. Choose ONE important **character** from the film you studied and explain how he or she was influenced by the world in which they lived.

4. Describe the **opening scene** in the film you studied and explain how the director used that opening scene to draw the audience into the story, catch their attention and engage their interest. In your answer, you could refer to the rough notes you make in the grid below. You may substitute headings as appropriate to your film:

Characters	
Costume or appearance	
Setting in time	

Setting in place	
Sounds/music	
Words/voices	

5. Choose ONE **key moment** from the film you studied and describe the impact it had on you. In your answer you could refer to the rough notes you make in the grid below :

Characters	
Costume or appearance	
Setting in time	
Setting in place	
Sounds/music	
Words/voices	

Remember!

A **key moment** will often be chosen as a trailer to promote the film. It may be a moment of great excitement, drama or emotional intensity, accompanied by music or sound effects that add to the mood. A key moment may advance the plot, create atmosphere or give us an understanding of theme, characters or the world the characters live in. It is always a special moment that can be magical, memorable or mesmerising.

Write for a Variety of Purposes

Write Descriptively

Students should be able to:

Write for a variety of purposes, for example to analyse, evaluate, imagine, explore, engage, amuse, narrate, inform, explain, argue, persuade.

(Final Examination Requirement: English Specification, 15)

Scrooge, in Charles Dickens's *A Christmas Carol*, hated Christmas jollity. He lived a lonely, miserable life until one Christmas, when he was visited by the ghost of Jacob Marley.

Complete the paragraph below, using appropriate **adjectives**, **nouns** and **verbs** to describe Scrooge's first meeting with the ghost of his dead partner.

It is Christmas Eve and an ______________________ wind blows through London.

______________________ , ______________________ Scrooge is ______________________

by a ______________________ fire in his ______________________ sitting room. Suddenly, he

hears the sound of the cellar door ______________________ open. A ______________________

noise, like someone ______________________ a chain across a ______________________

floor, ______________________ through the house. The sound of ______________________

footsteps ______________________ him and he ______________________ with

______________________.

He turns abruptly to see the ______________________ face of Jacob Marley, with its

______________________ eyes, laden down with ______________________ chains, padlocks

and cash boxes.

Who are you?

In life, I was your partner, Jacob Marley.

Write to Create Tension or Suspense

Write a paragraph in a story in which you use **verbs**, **adjectives**, **adverbs** and phrases that create an atmosphere of suspense.

Tip

Think of a paragraph in a novel or short story that was full of suspense. Reread that paragraph to get ideas for character, situation, and vocabulary.

Write to Narrate – A Novel Opening

Students should be able to:

Engage in the writing process as a private, pleasurable and purposeful activity ... using a personal voice as their individual style is thoughtfully developed.

(Final Examination Requirement: English Specification, 15)

- Choose one of the sentences below.
- Fill in the gaps with either a word or a phrase.
- Write further sentences to complete a paragraph.
- Read it aloud to the person or group beside you.
- Give the paragraph a mark out of 10.
- Defend your mark with a comment that explains why you gave that mark. For example:

This paragraph makes the listener or reader curious to read on/uses good vocabulary/ clearly describes a time and place/has an atmosphere that draws you in/creates interesting character(s).

Inspirational texts

The novel openings in the section **Responding to Texts** on pages 49–50

1. Beads of sweat dripped from ______________________'s forehead as the crowbar slowly prised open the heavy ______________________ of the ______________________. This was the perfect hiding place, near the junkyards, the yelping guard dogs and putrid smells of diesel, kerosene and burnt tyres.

(__/10)

2. As light snowflakes fell softly from a starry sky, a huddle of weary shadows crept in single file through the ____________________, avoiding roadblocks and checkpoints, desperate to reach the ____________________ before daybreak.

____

____

____

____

____

____ (__/10)

3. 'Are you having a laugh?' the shaven-headed, hard-faced, massive-chested bouncer growled as ____________________ tried to slink in behind ____________________ and ____________________. 'Read the notice.' *Under 12s must be accompanied by an adult.* 'Go home, sonny, and get your mammy.'

____

____

____

____

____

____ (__/10)

4. Write an opening paragraph of your own.

____

____

____

____

____

____

____

____

____

____

____ (__/10)

Write to Inform – A Media Broadcast

Students should be able to:

Write for a variety of purposes, for example to .... inform.

(Final Examination Requirement: English Specification, 15)

Read the following radio news item, which is written in formal broadcasting language. Fill in the gaps to give a specific location.

Reports are coming in of a major incident occurring at this moment in ______________________
We are hearing reports that a 4×4 car has been driven at speed along the pavement heading towards
______________________.

Eye-witness reports say that this vehicle mowed down several ______________________ before crashing into railings. A man ______________________ with a knife is said to have left the car and entered ______________________. Sounds thought to be gunfire have been heard and we have unconfirmed reports that an unarmed police officer was attacked, perhaps fatally. We will continue to bring you news as it comes in.

Language

This report uses carefully chosen words and phrases to tell listeners that the news station is as yet uncertain of the facts. Quote **three words or phrases** in the text that tell listeners that this news is as yet unconfirmed.

1. ____
2. ____
3. ____

The Five Ws

The report gives listeners the **what**, **where**, **when**, **who** of this incident (We don't yet know **why** it has happened). When you have filled in the gaps above, write complete sentences in the spaces below.

WHAT has happened?

____

WHERE has it happened?

____

WHEN has it happened or is continuing to happen?

____

WHO is involved or affected by what is happening?

____

Breaking the news

Plan a breaking news broadcast about an incident that is happening at this moment. Reports, as yet unconfirmed, are coming into the newsroom …

WHAT has happened?

____

WHERE has it happened?

____

WHEN has it happened or is continuing to happen?

____

WHO is involved or affected by what is happening?

____

Write the report you would broadcast at this stage.

Rough Work

____

____

____

____

____

____

____

____

____

Write to inform of confirmed facts

Imagine that a group of tourists (e.g. in a hotel/on a holiday island), have been taken hostage by heavily armed captors demanding a ransom. A small team of special operatives has been sent in to free the hostages.

Write the script for a news broadcast reporting the success or failure of this mission to free the hostages.

Tip

A news item must include the five Ws: Who? What? Where? When? Why?

This is a headline story, so you could begin with, *'Good evening. News is coming in of …'*

Rough Work

Write a Speech – Use Appropriate Vocabulary, Style and Tone to Suit Purpose and Audience

Inspiring others

Students should be able to:

Write competently in a range of text forms ... using appropriate vocabulary, tone ... to achieve a chosen purpose.

(Final Examination Requirement: English Specification, 15)

Engage with and learn from models of oral and written language use to enrich their own written work.

(English Specification, 15)

Now imagine that you are the commander of the team of special operatives sent in to save the hostages (see page 109) You know that there is great risk. Your aim is to avoid loss of life.

Write the short speech that you would make to this small force, which would motivate them and inspire them to successfully carry out this mission.

Inspirational texts

Eisenhower's speech on page 37.

King Henry's speech to his troops at Agincourt in Shakespeare's *Henry V*, page 142.

Rough Work

Reflect on your writing

Point out **two** elements in your speech that would make an impact on the men and women who are about to go on this mission.

Write to Engage and Persuade

Promotional press release

You have just made a documentary (either film or audio) about a person in public life, in sport or in the world of entertainment.

Write a promotional press release telling viewers or listeners that this is a must-see programme that they will find informative and enjoyable. Give your documentary a title.

Inspirational text

RTÉ promotional press release advertising a documentary on the O'Donovan brothers (page 40). Note that RTÉ gave their documentary a catchy, appealing title – an important documentary technique.

Give your documentary an interesting title that will catch the attention of listeners or viewers.

Use appropriate register, vocabulary, images, humour, appealing story, etc. as RTÉ did.

Suggest a photograph that would give added appeal and attract an audience for the programme.

Rough Work

Reflect on your writing

Point out **two aspects** of your press release that would attract an audience to the programme

TV spot

Write the introduction to a new television show, in which you are the presenter whose first job is to invite viewers to become participants in the show.

Inspirational text

See Sample Paper 2: Presenter calling on viewers to audition for a talent show (page 149).

Rough Work

Reflect on your writing

Point out **two aspects** of your press release that would attract viewers to become participants in your show.

Write to Inform

Students should be able to:

Use a wide range of reading comprehension strategies appropriate to texts ... to retrieve information.

(English Specification, 14)

Read the Census 2016 infographic below.

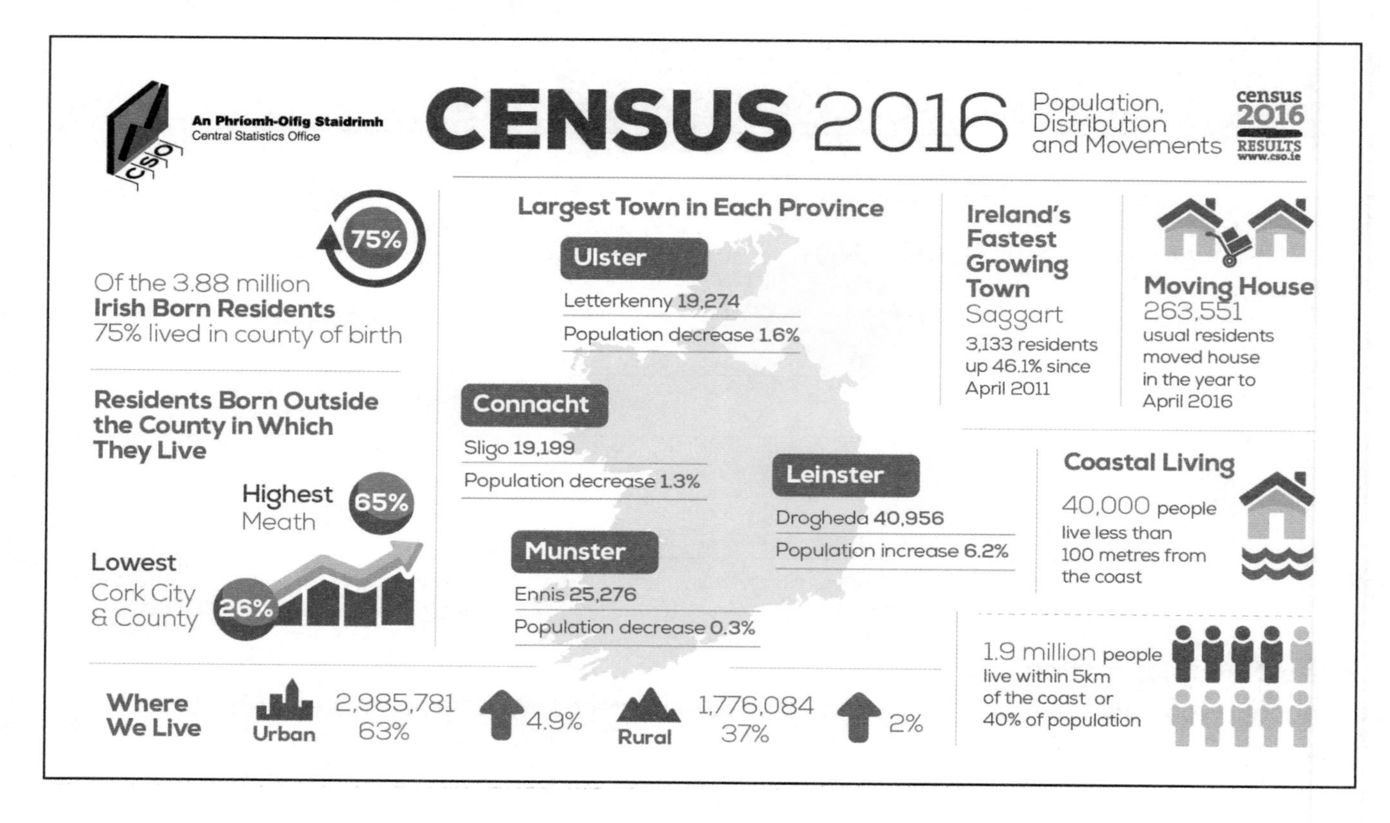

Write the information in this infographic in the form of a talk to a group of students and their teachers from abroad who are visiting your school.

As you speak, you have the infographic up on the screen beside you and are pointing out the facts. (You can download it from www.cso.ie – click on 'Visualisation Tools', then on 'Infographic Data Visualisation', then scroll down to the 'Census' section.) Instead of giving statements only, you could turn the facts into questions, so your listeners have to think before you tell them the facts. An example would be: Where do you think the fastest growing population is?

Tip

It is important to make your talk interesting and to avoid simply listing the information.

Try to use phrases like:

You might be surprised to hear that ...

Irish people move around this country less than you would think ...

Ireland is surrounded by water; therefore you will notice that ...

Can you guess which ... ?

Full Sample Examination Papers

In this section of the book, you will practise the skills needed for a full examination paper.

Each sample answer has a side panel giving you the examiner's comments.

Tip

Continue to develop your examination skills by writing your own answer ***before*** you read the sample answer.

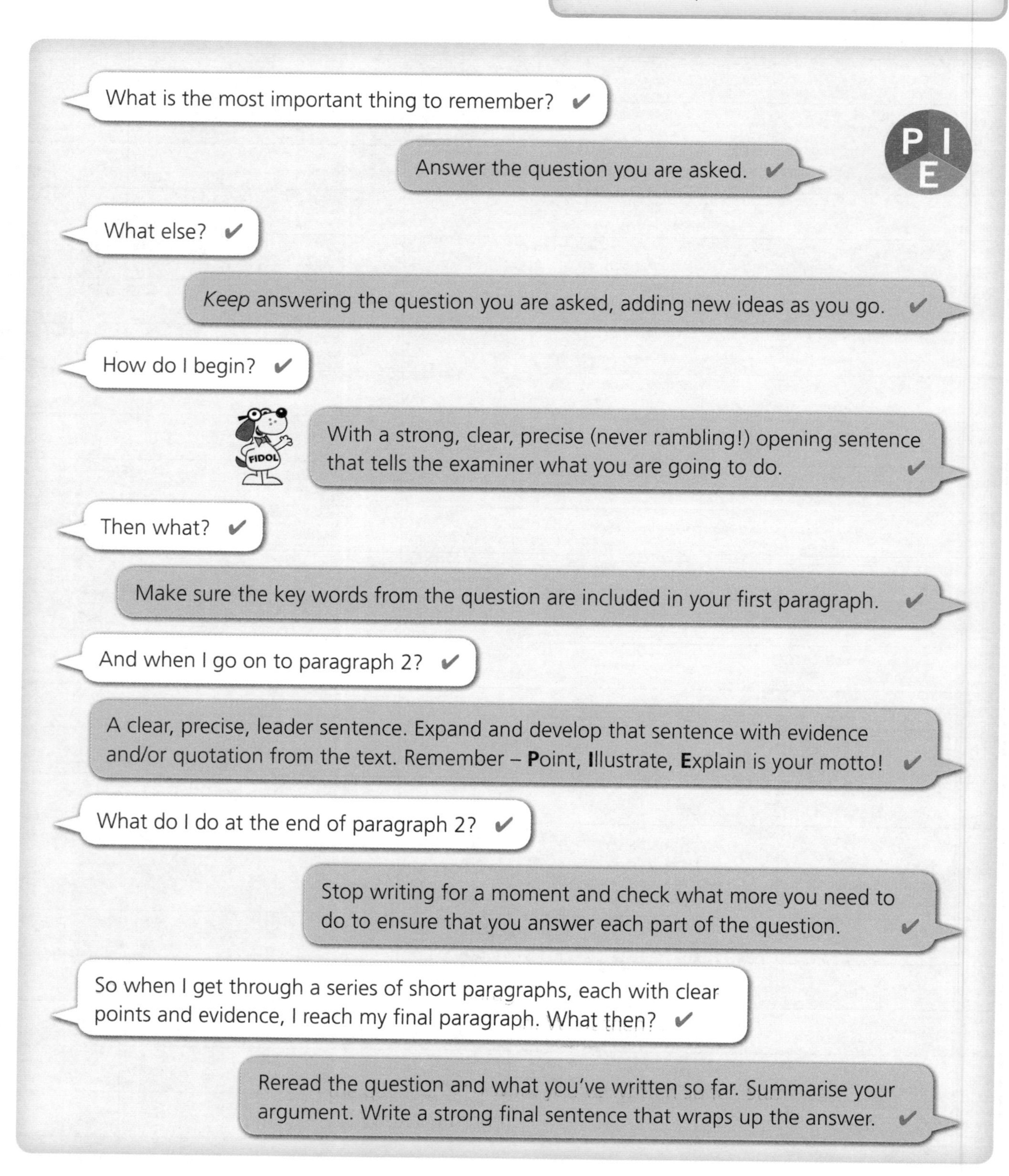

What New Skills do I Need for a Full Paper?

1. Timing

- You have **120 minutes** to answer all of the questions on the paper.
- The instructions on page 1 of the paper give you timings for each answer. Use the first five minutes to read the questions and plan your timings.
- On the **Instructions** page, write the start times to the right of each section. See the example on page 124.

2. Expect the unexpected!

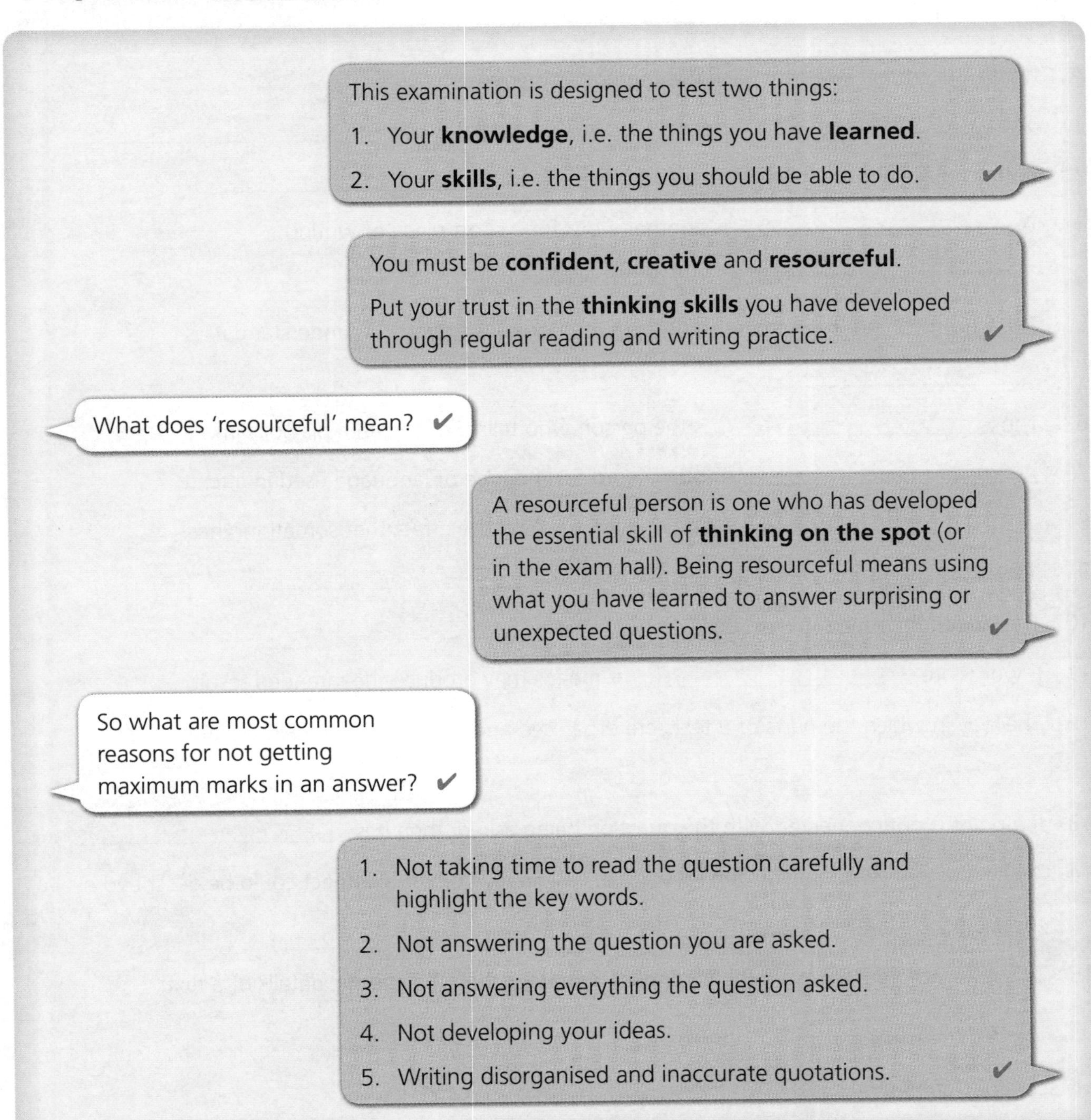

Key Vocabulary for the Examination

Certain important words come up regularly in the Higher Level examination.

Test yourself on examination vocabulary using the following exercises:

Analyse	Passage	Register
Dialogue	Setting	Structure
Extract	Engaging	Texts
Effective	Impact	Gist
Striking	Irrelevant	Narrator

A. Choose the correct word for each of the phrases below.

1. The word used in the exam for novels, plays, poems and extracts is ____________________.
2. A short piece chosen from a literary text is called an ____________________.
3. A ____________________ is another word for a short piece of writing.
4. The time and place in which a story occurs is called the ____________________.
5. The verb meaning 'to examine something methodically so you can understand it' is ____________________.
6. The ____________________ is the person who tells the story in a play or film.
7. ____________________ is another word for the type of language used in a text.
8. ____________________ is a single word meaning the effect that something has.
9. If a text is interesting and enjoyable, we say it is ____________________.
10. The word for conversation in a play is ____________________.
11. If words are ____________________, it means they produce the intended result.
12. The way in which the parts of a texts are organised and put together is called the ____________________.
13. If a point is not connected with the question being asked, then it is ____________________.
14. A key moment which has strong emotional, imaginative or visual impact could be described by the word ____________________.
15. This little word describes the general meaning rather than the specific details of a text: ____________________.

My score out of **15** marks is _____.

Caption	Adapted	Prose
Justify	Accurate	In context
Author	Aspects	Infographic
Technique	Communicate	Contrasting
Qualities	Significant	Evaluate

B. Choose the correct word for each of the phrases below.

1. A ______________________ is a poet's creative or clever way of using words.
2. Information written below a photograph is called the ______________________.
3. The general word for a writer of plays, poems, novels, etc. is ______________________.
4. Language that is not poetry is called ______________________.
5. A graphic display of information that uses words and visuals is called an ______________________.
6. ______________________ is comparing texts in order to highlight differences.
7. The verb '______________________' means to look for qualities in a text and form an opinion.
8. We could substitute the word ______________________ for 'convey' in the phrase:

   What words best convey the writer's message?
9. Which word in the following sentence means 'features' or 'parts'? ______________________

   Refer to aspects of the script to support your answer.
10. Another word for 'absolutely correct' is ______________________.
11. The features to be admired in a person, thing or text are called ______________________.
12. ______________________ means to give proof or a good reason for your opinion.
13. ______________________ means in a particular time, place or situation or set of circumstances.
14. ______________________ means slightly changed or simplified.
15. If something is ______________________, it is important and should be noted.

My score out of **15** marks is _____.

My total score out of **30** marks is _____.

Sample Paper 1

The theme of this examination paper is Journeys

Plan your timings before you start answering the questions!

Instructions

There are four sections in this examination paper.

Section A	Reading to analyse and evaluate	50 marks	3 questions	09.35
Section B	Responding to texts	55 marks	4 questions	10.05
Section C	Showing critical appreciation	55 marks	2 questions	10.40
Section D	Reading comprehension strategies	20 marks	2 questions	11.15

Answer all questions.

The questions do not all carry equal marks. The number of marks for each question is stated at the top of the question.

You should spend about 30 minutes on Section A, 35 minutes on Section B, 35 minutes on Section C, and 15 minutes on Section D.

When answering on studied material, you must use texts in line with what is prescribed for your course.

Section A — Reading to analyse and evaluate — 50 marks

The following script is taken from a radio documentary called *Don't Go Far*. The full documentary was broadcast as part of the RTÉ Radio *Documentary on One* series. It tells a story from 1985 when two young Dublin boys took a DART to Dun Laoghaire and then travelled without tickets as far as New York. Keith Byrne, now in his 30s, was 10 at the time of this journey. This documentary has won many international awards.

FX: People talking and sound of train door beeping alarm

Narrator: Dublin, August 1985.

FX: Train door beeping

Narrator: Two Dubliners on the DART (Dublin Area Rapid Transit). This is the new suburban rail system – just opened.

FX: DART train (electric) moving – sound of wheels on tracks.

Narrator: It has changed their lives. They could now venture far afield from their home in Darndale, North Dublin.

FX: DART train sound fades out

Keith Byrne: We used to always get on the DART and go out to Bray [seaside resort 20 km south of Darndale] and go out to Dun Laoghaire [Dublin suburb/ferry port 10 km south of Darndale] and … so these were all kind of new places so we just, and then, we realised that there was a boat, the ferry [car/

passenger ferry], that went from Dun Laoghaire over to England, so that was an extended version of the adventure if you like.

FX: DART train on tracks

Keith: We went over a couple of times, like, we used to do this kinda on a regular thing, we'd go over to bunk (hide) on the ferry over to England and then go from there, jump on a train or coach or whatever and go on an adventure.

FX: Train doors

Narrator: That's Keith Byrne, talking about heading off with a couple of friends. But that's Keith Byrne *now*. In 1985, when he was getting the DART to Dun Laoghaire and sneaking on the ferry to England, Keith was 10 [years old].

FX: Ferry boat horn

Music: Song » Lloyd Cole & The Commotions » Lost Weekend

Narrator: So, Keith Byrne, aged 10, and his friend, Noel Murray, aged 13 are sitting on the DART train into town [Dublin city centre]. But the town they're heading for isn't Dublin, in fact, it isn't even in Ireland. Keith and Noel's final destination is so far away and the story of their epic journey there causes such a fuss that within a couple of days, these two boys – sitting on a Dublin train – in August 1985, will become front page news.

FX: DART Train on tracks

Morning Ireland presenter (from radio archive, 1985): This is 'Morning Ireland' [the largest radio news show in Ireland]. It's a quarter past eight [8.15am]. The news headlines, two Dublin boys ...

Newsreader (from archive, 1985): The news headlines: Two Dublin boys, aged 10 and 13, have been returned to Ireland after stowing away ... [Fade out]

Question 1 — 20 marks

From your reading of this script, point out some of the imaginative ways in which this radio documentary tells a story and engages the radio audience.

Rough Work

Question 2 **15 marks**

From your reading of the introduction and extract, what elements of this story do you think would be appealing to a radio audience?

Rough Work

ONE MILLION people to flee Mosul as Iraqi troops and coalition forces try to force ISIS out

Question 3 **15 marks**

Write a critical analysis of this photograph, explaining how you think it adds to the impact of the newspaper headline.

Rough Work

Section B	Responding to texts – Appreciating language	55 marks

Read the text printed below and the extract from Shakespeare's play, ***As You Like It***. Answer the questions which follow.

> Jacques is a gloomy, pessimistic character in the play ***As You Like It***. In this soliloquy, he gives us his view on life. He thinks it is like a play divided into seven sad scenes, from the cradle to the grave.
>
> Babies are a crying, needy nuisances; young men are rash and stupid, middle-aged men are fat, powerful people become greedy and take bribes; old age is weak, pathetic and ridiculous.

Jaques:

All the world's a stage,
And all the men and women merely players:
They have their exits and their entrances
And one man in his time plays many parts,
His acts being seven ages. At first the infant,
Mewling and puking in the nurse's arms; — *crying and getting sick*
Then, the whining schoolboy with his satchel
And shining morning face, creeping like snail
Unwillingly to school; and then the lover,
Sighing like furnace, with a woeful ballad
Made to his mistress' eyebrow; then a soldier,
Full of strange oaths and bearded like the pard, — *leopard*
Jealous in honour, sudden, and quick in quarrel, — *egotistical about his reputation*
Seeking the bubble 'reputation'
Even in the cannon's mouth; and then the justice,
In fair round belly with good capon lined, — *good meat*

With eyes severe and beard of formal cut,
Full of wise saws and modern instances – *clever sayings*
And so he plays his part; the sixth age shifts
Into the lean and slippered pantaloon, *baggy trousers*
With spectacles on nose and pouch on side,
His youthful hose well saved – a world too wide
For his shrunk shank – and his big manly voice, *skinny legs*
Turning again toward childish treble, pipes *squeaky, high voice*
And whistles in his sound; last scene of all,
That ends this strange eventful history
Is second childishness and mere oblivion, *forgetfulness nothingness*
Sans teeth, sans eyes, sans taste, sans everything.

Question 4 **5 * 3 marks**

Write the letter corresponding to the correct answer in the box.

(a) The opening line is an example of
A. Simile
B. Metaphor
C. Personification

☐

(b) The young boyfriend
A. Is a great poet
B. Writes stupid poems
C. Takes it easy

☐

(c) The soldier
A. Is slow to anger
B. Is clean-shaven
C. Is willing to lose his life for glory

☐

(d) The middle-aged judge
A. Is a fat, corrupt know-all
B. Eats very little
C. Has a rough beard

☐

(e) The elderly man
A. Wears smart shoes
B. Is only a thin shadow of his former strong self
C. Has a strong, manly voice

☐

Question 5 **10 marks**

Choose **two** of the seven ages described by Jaques.

In the case of each choice, describe how you think the actor might use voice, facial expression, a dramatic gesture or movement and/or a prop in order to perform this speech in an imaginative way.

Rough Work

Question 6 **5 marks**

This famous speech has a great impact on the theatre audience when it is spoken on stage. Point to a speech in your studied play that you think would have a great impact on the audience when it is spoken on stage.

Title of play: ____________________

The memorable speech about ____________________ spoken by

____

Question 7 **25 marks**

Explain what the speech you have chosen says to the audience and describe how you think the actor might use voice, facial expression, a dramatic gesture or movement and/or a prop in order to perform this speech in an imaginative way.

Rough Work

Section C Showing critical appreciation – Poetic use of language 55 marks

Read the following poem by Siegfried Sassoon and answer the questions that follow:

The General

'Good-morning, good-morning!' the General said

When we met him last week on our way to the line.

Now the soldiers he smiled at are most of 'em dead,

And we're cursing his staff for incompetent swine.

'He's a cheery old card,' grunted Harry to Jack

As they slogged up to Arras with rifle and pack.

But he did for them both by his plan of attack.

Question 8 4 * 5 marks

Identify a line or lines in the poem where the poet uses each of the following poetic techniques.

Rhyming couplet

____

____

Assonance

____

____

Alliteration

____

____

Effective use of pause

____

____

Question 9 – Your studied poems

35 marks

Choose any two poems you have studied that told a story about a journey.

Give the poets' names and the titles of the poems.

Give full titles and names with correct spelling.

Title Poem 1:	Title Poem 2:
Poet's name:	Poet's name:

In your opinion, which of the two poems told the most interesting story and which used language in the most imaginative way? Give reasons for your opinions.

Rough Work

Section D — Reading comprehension strategies — 20 marks

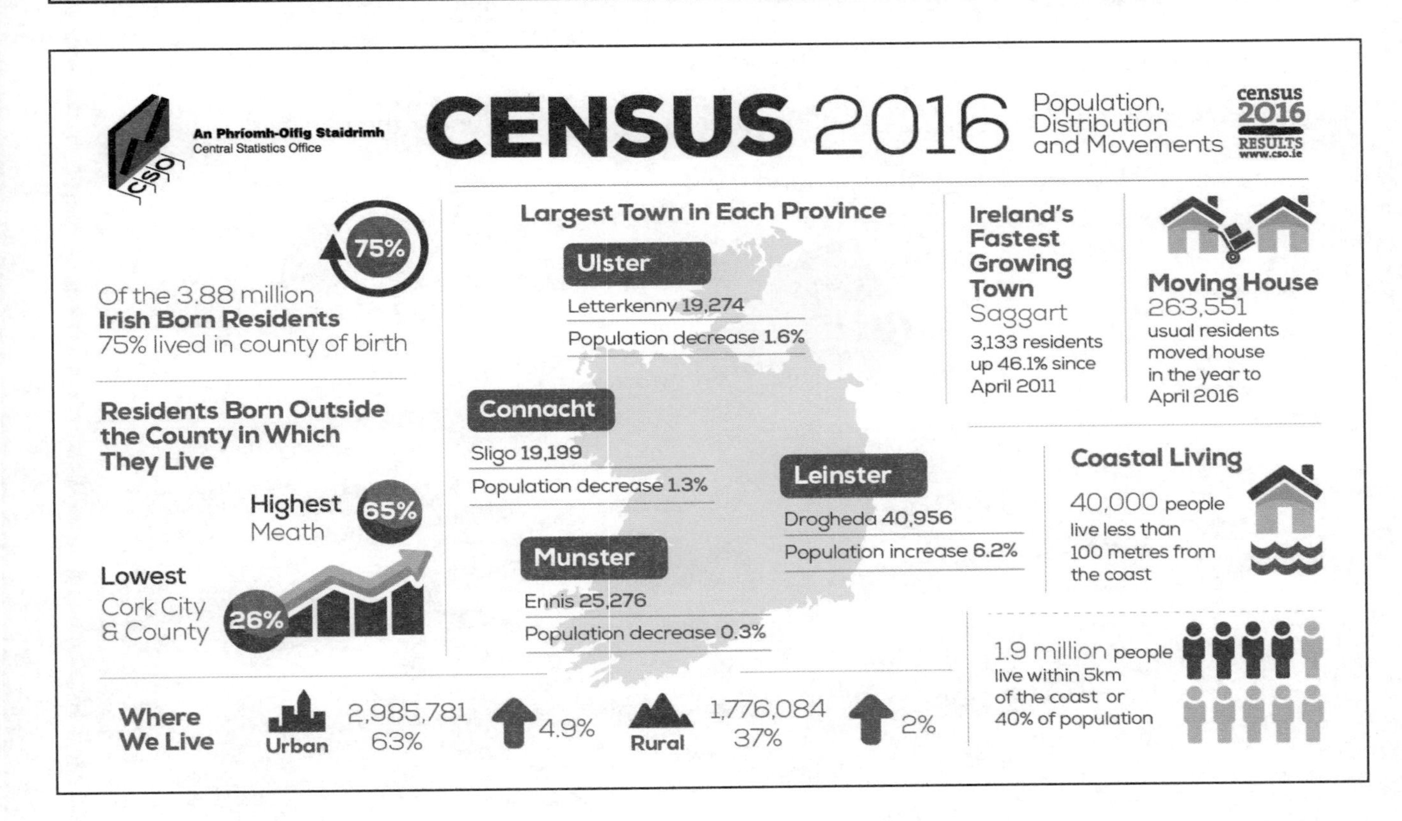

Question 10 **10 marks**

Study the above infographic on Ireland's population, distribution and movements, then complete the following sentences.

Name the state agency that has published these figures.

What percentage of Irish-born residents no longer live in the county in which they were born?

___

'The population is growing faster in cities than in the countryside.' Is this true or false?

___

'More than half the population lives more than 5 km from the coast.' Is this true or false?

___

'6.2% is the greatest population increase in a town in Ireland in the years between 2011 and 2016.' Is this true or false?

___

Question 11 **10 marks**

Write the correct version of the homophone in each case

The qu___ ___ ___ suburban village of Saggart now has qu___ ___ ___ a large population.

The audience had not yet s___ ___ ___ the last s___ ___n___ in the play.

We heard a loud b___ ___ ___ when the toddler lost his b___ ___ ___.

The children searched for th___ ___ ___ shoes over th___ ___ ___ under the benches.

The game will be played w___ ___ther or not the w___ ___ther is good.

Sample Paper 2

The theme of this examination paper is Persuasion

Instructions

There are three sections in this examination paper.

Timing

Section A	Reading texts to understand – Shakespearean drama	75 marks	4 questions	09.35
Section B	Appreciating audience and register	40 marks	2 questions	10.20
Section C	Responding to studied texts	65 marks	3 questions	10.50

Answer all questions.

The questions do not all carry equal marks. The number of marks for each question is stated at the top of the question.

You should spend about 45 minutes on Section A, 30 minutes on Section B and 40 minutes on Section C.

When answering on studied material, you must use texts in line with what is prescribed for your course.

Section A Reading texts to understand – Shakespearean drama 75 marks

See the extract below from Shakespeare's play ***Henry V.***

Background

It is 1415, 25th October, feast of Saint Crispian. This is King Henry V's speech to his outnumbered, exhausted English army who are about to fight the French army at the Battle of Agincourt. He tells them that they are all brothers and though they are few in number, they are strong. In time to come, they will be proud to say they were here at this moment and that they fought and won this battle.

Henry himself led his army into this battle. His English and Welsh longbow archers rained black showers of arrows on the French cavalry. This day became one of the most famous victories in English history. Legend says that they lost only 400 men, while the French lost 7,000.

Henry:

He that hath no stomach to this fight,

Let him depart …

We would not die in that man's company …

This day is called the feast of Crispian.
He that outlives this day, and comes safe home,
Will stand a tip-toe when this day is named,
And rouse him at the name of Crispian.
He that shall live this day, and see old age,
Will yearly on the vigil feast his neighbours,
And say 'To-morrow is Saint Crispian:'
Then will he strip his sleeve and show his scars,
And say 'These wounds I had on Crispian's day …'

This story shall the good man teach his son;
We few, we happy few, we band of brothers;
For he to-day that sheds his blood with me
Shall be my brother; …

And gentlemen in England now a-bed
Shall think themselves accursed they were not here,
And hold their manhoods cheap whiles any speaks
That fought with us upon Saint Crispin's day.

Question 1 **5 * 3 marks**

(a) Which one of the following is the best explanation of the line

He that hath no stomach to this fight

A. Anyone who is hungry
B. Anyone who is afraid to go into battle
C. This battle will be easy

☐

(b) Which one of the following is the best explanation of the lines

He that outlives this day, and comes safe home,
Will stand a tip-toe when this day is named

A. Soldiers who survive this day will be proud for ever
B. The tallest will survive
C. Fight bravely and live

☐

(c) What does Henry mean when he says that people who listen to the soldiers will 'hold their manhoods cheap'?

A. They will feel proud
B. They will hold up banners
C. They will feel inferior to the soldiers who fought here

☐

(d) Which idea of war does the speech support?

A. War can never be justified
B. Victory in war is great and glorious
C. Old soldiers are forgotten

☐

(e) Which adjectives best describe Henry's mood as he finished his speech?

A. Anxious, secretive and cautious
B. Timid, reserved and shy
C. Jubilant, confident and optimistic

☐

Question 2

Select one character from a Shakespearean play you have studied and list five adjectives that describe this character.

Title of play:

____

Name of character:

____

5 marks

Five adjectives

1. ______________________________
2. ______________________________
3. ______________________________
4. ______________________________
5. ______________________________

15 marks

Choose **one** of the qualities identified in your list above. Explain how this quality is shown in a key moment from the play.

Rough Work

Question 3

20 marks

This poster was used by the BBC to advertise their film version of ***Henry V***.

Write a critical analysis of the poster above.

In your analysis you should consider:

- The visual impact of the poster

and

- Whether or not the poster makes you want to see the film.

Rough Work

Question 4 **20 marks**

If you were asked to design a poster to advertise a BBC performance of your studied play, what would you show on this poster? You are aiming to make a strong visual impact and to attract a wide audience. Consider visual images, contrast, character, colours, quotation etc., as in the ***Henry V*** poster on page 145.

The examiner expects you to analyse aspects of the poster and to deal with both of the prompts, but not necessarily equally. You may or may not want to see the film.

Rough Work

Section B	Appreciating audience and register	40 marks

In this introduction to a new television show, the presenter invites viewers to audition for a talent contest.

> People of Ireland, listen up. Think you've got what it takes to be a star? Reckon you could be the next big thing selling millions of records worldwide and dazzling audiences in London, Dubai, New York or Sydney? The show is open to any performer of any age, from any background: all you need is the star quality that will impress the judges. We are searching for the best talent in the land, because we know that the talent level here is sky-high!
>
> Are you ready to meet the judges? Can you wow our live audience? If you wannabe the next superstar, this is your moment. Live your dream! WE are giving YOU the opportunity to showcase and shine! Get ready to conquer the world. Get yourself down here next Saturday for an open day of auditioning for the next series of WOW!

Question 5 **20 marks**

In your opinion, what elements of the text above would engage listeners and persuade them to become participants in the show?

Rough Work

Question 6

Read this extract from the 1916 Proclamation.

> IRISHMEN AND IRISHWOMEN: In the name of God and of the dead generations from which she receives her old tradition of nationhood, Ireland, through us, summons her children to her flag and strikes for her freedom …
>
> The Irish Republic is entitled to, and hereby claims, the allegiance of every Irishman and Irishwoman. The Republic guarantees religious and civil liberty, equal rights and equal opportunities to all its citizens, and declares its resolve to pursue the happiness and prosperity of the whole nation and of all its parts, cherishing all of the children of the nation equally, and oblivious of the differences carefully fostered by an alien Government, which have divided a minority from the majority in the past.

Compare and contrast the purpose, language and style of this speech with the television script in question 5 on page 149.

20 marks

Rough Work

Section C Responding to studied texts – Novel and short story 65 marks

Question 7 – Your studied novel 30 marks

Write a pitch to a film producer, persuading him or her that a novel that you have studied on your course has the potential to become a great film.

From your STUDIED NOVELS, choose ONE.

Title of novel	Author

Rough Work

Question 8 **25 marks**

A film is being made of a novel you have studied.

What would you include on a poster advertising the film? It should represent what you think is important in the film, and persuade the audience to see it. Explain your decisions with reference to the novel.

Novel	Author

Rough Work

Question 9 **10 marks**

Fill in the gaps in the words that are commonly misspelled:

(a) I will defin__________ly remember the princip__________s I was taught by my parents.

(b) Your lack of __________nowle__________e of gra__________r should never di__________point or embar__________ you.

(c) I love the musical r__________hm at the beg__________ing and ending of this poem about autu__________.

(d) The gover__________ent declared that all the educational changes were ne__________sary in order to ac__________ve suc__________s.

(e) I bel__________ve that you dec__________ved us with a false rec__________pt for the damaged c__________ling.

(f) Our school princip__________ t__________ght us the importance of good behav__________r.

Sample Paper 3

The theme of this examination paper is Change

Instructions

There are three sections in this examination paper.

Timing

Section A	Responding to texts – Key moments	80 marks	4 questions	09.35
Section B	Reading comprehension strategies	30 marks	2 questions	10.25
Section C	Reading texts to understand – Shakespeare	70 marks	4 questions	10.40

Answer all questions.

The questions do not all carry equal marks. The number of marks for each question is stated at the top of the question.

You should spend about 50 minutes on Section A, 15 minutes on Section B and 50 minutes on Section C.

When answering on studied material, you must use texts in line with what is prescribed for your course.

Section A — Responding to texts – Key moments — 80 marks

Read the the background text and the closing extract from Frank O'Connor's story, 'Guests of the Nation'. Answer the questions that follow.

Background

The story is set during the War of Independence between the Irish Republican Army and the British security forces in Ireland. The narrator, a young man who is a member of the IRA, is part of a group holding two British soldiers hostage in a cottage in a remote bogland. He has just witnessed them being taken out and shot as a reprisal and has helped to bury them in the bogland.

Hostages and captors had played cards together and chatted at the fire every evening, never imagining that a moment would come when there would be an execution order. This closing scene occurs at night as they return to the cottage and are questioned by the old woman who has been their housekeeper.

Characters

- The narrator
- An old woman who lives in the cottage where the hostages were being held
- Noble, one of the IRA men holding the two hostages

She rose quietly and came to the doorway with all her cantankerousness gone.

'What did ye do with them?' she asked in a whisper, and Noble started so that the match went out in his hand.

'What's that?' he asked without turning around.

'I heard ye,' she said.

'What did you hear?' asked Noble.

'I heard ye. Do you think I didn't hear ye putting the spade back in the houseen?'

I stood at the door, watching the stars and listening to the shrieking of the birds dying out over the bogs. It is so strange what you feel at times like that that you can't describe it. Noble says he saw everything ten times the size, as though there were nothing in the whole world but that little patch of bog with the two Englishmen stiffening into it, but with me it was as if the patch of bog where the Englishmen were was a million miles away, and even Noble and the old woman, mumbling behind me, and the birds and the bloody stars were all far away, and I was somehow very small and very lost and lonely like a child astray in the snow. And anything that happened to me afterwards, I never felt the same about again.

Question 1 **30 marks**

(a) How does the setting for this scene create mood or atmosphere? (10 marks)

(b) A key moment is a scene or moment of great emotional intensity that often illuminates character and makes a strong impact on the reader. In light of this definition, what aspects of this closing scene make it a key moment? (20 marks)

Rough Work

Question 2

From your STUDIED SHORT STORIES or your STUDIED NOVEL, name the ONE that you most enjoyed reading for the first time, and then rereading.

Title of short story or novel	Author

20 marks

Explain why you enjoyed reading this story for the first time, and why you enjoyed rereading it.

Rough Work

Question 3 **20 marks**

Write about ONE key moment in your chosen short story or novel, explaining what made it a key moment.

Rough Work

Question 4 **10 marks**

The following words and phrases appear in the passage. Write a definition of each word **as it is used in the passage**.

Cantankerousness

Started

Shrieking

Mumbling

Astray

Section B	Reading comprehension strategies	30 marks

Study the August 2017 homepage of **Basketball Ireland** below and answer the questions that follow.

Question 5 **10 marks**

(a) Identify two digital elements used in the above screenshot from the Basketball Ireland website.

	Digital element
1.	
2.	

10 marks

(b) What impression of Basketball Ireland is made in this moment on their homepage and how is that impression communicated in both images and text?

Question 6 **10 marks**

If you were asked to design a website for your sport, hobby or any organisation in which you were involved,

(a) What digital elements would be essential on your page?

(b) What information would you give to users?

(c) What images would you place on the homepage?

(d) What text or headlines would you place in order to catch and hold web users' attention and interest?

Section C	Reading texts to understand	70 marks

Julius Caesar Act IV Scene (ii)

Read the text printed below and the extract from Shakespeare's play, ***Julius Caesar***. Answer the questions which follow.

Background

Shakespeare's play ***Julius Caesar*** is a tragedy based on the assassination of Caesar and the fate of those who conspired in his downfall. Julius Caesar is assassinated by a group of conspirators led by Cassius and Brutus, who said he was becoming too powerful and therefore should be feared as a ruler. The assassination caused a civil war.

Now a great battle is about to take place, but Brutus suspects that Cassius has changed towards him. He is not as close and loyal to him as he pretended to be when he convinced him to take part in the assassination. He now thinks that Cassius may fail them when put to the test. He uses a simile referring to horses in battle to describe a cooling friendship.

When Cassius arrives with most of his army he immediately accuses Brutus of having wronged him. Brutus responds that he would not wrong a friend and suggests that they talk inside his tent so that 'both our armies' will not see them quarrelling. Brutus believes Cassius has been selling promises of jobs in the new government in return for bribes.

Brutus:

He is not doubted. A word, Lucilius; *Lucilius is the messenger who went to speak to Cassius*
How he received you, let me be resolved.

Lucilius:

With courtesy and with respect enough;
But not with such familiar instances,
Nor with such free and friendly conference,
As he hath used of old.

Brutus:

Thou hast described
A hot friend cooling: ever note, Lucilius,
When love begins to sicken and decay,
It useth an enforced ceremony.
There are no tricks in plain and simple faith;
But hollow men, like horses hot at hand,
Make gallant show and promise of their mettle;
But when they should endure the bloody spur,
They fall their crests, and, like deceitful jades, *like worthless horses*
Sink in the trial.

...

Brutus:
Hark! he is arrived.

Enter CASSIUS

…

Cassius:
Most noble brother, you have done me wrong.

Brutus:
Judge me, you gods! Wrong I mine enemies?
And, if not so, how should I wrong a brother?

…

Speak your griefs softly: I do know you well.
Before the eyes of both our armies here,
Which should perceive nothing but love from us,
Let us not wrangle: bid them move away;
Then in my tent, Cassius, enlarge your griefs,
And I will give you audience.

…

(Brutus's tent.)

Cassius:
You have condemned and noted Lucius Pella
For taking bribes here of the Sardians …

Brutus:
Let me tell you, Cassius, you yourself
Are much condemned to have an itching palm,
To sell and mart your offices for gold
To undeservers.

Cassius:
I an itching palm?
You know that you are Brutus that speaks this,
Or, by the gods, this speech were else your last …

Brutus:
Remember March, the ides of March remember.
Did not great Julius bleed for justice' sake?
What villain touched his body, that did stab,
And not for justice? What, shall one of us,
That struck the foremost man of all this world
But for supporting robbers, shall we now
Contaminate our fingers with base bribes?

Question 7 **5 * 3 marks**

Find phrases in the extract that are closest to the following modern English phrases

(a) Easy, cheerful chatter

(b) It becomes artificially polite and insincere

(c) Sincere people don't play games

(d) Don't shout your complaints

(e) Take money in exchange for job promises

Question 8 **3 * 5 marks**

(a) Write the metaphor that describes people who are full of hot air, brave talk and empty promises about what they are prepared to do.

(b) Write the line in which Cassius threatens Brutus.

(c) Briefly write Brutus' final words to Cassius in modern English.

Question 9 **10 marks**

From the play by Shakespeare that you studied, quote two lines that you enjoyed. Explain what the lines mean and state why you enjoyed them.

Question 10 **30 marks**

Select a scene from the Shakespearean play you studied in which two or more characters are in conflict.

Title of play: ______________________________

The conflict between ______________________________

Describe the scene. Describe how this conflict influenced your thoughts or feelings towards one of the characters involved.

Rough Work

Answers

Test your Critical Vocabulary

Introduction

Define five critical terms from examination papers to date.

1. **Aside**: a remark spoken by a character on stage which is meant to be heard by the audience, but not by other characters on stage.
2. **Assonance**: the repetition of vowel sounds in words that are spoken close together.
3. **Blank verse**: lines of unrhymed iambic pentameter, i.e. composed of ten syllables that are organised in five pairs. The first syllable is weak, the second stronger.
4. **Soliloquy**: a speech in which a character speaks to himself or herself, relating their deepest thoughts and feelings, sharing them with the audience, but not with other characters.
5. **Setting**: the time and place in which a poem, play, novel, story or film is set.

General Terms and Vocabulary

1. Characters; 2. Setting; 3. Costume; 4. Plot; 5. Protagonist; 6. Acts, Scenes; 7. Playwright, Dramatist; 8. Novelist; 9. Director; 10. Technique; 11. Monologue; 12. Documentary; 13. Extract; 14. Glossary; 15. Biography

Poetry

'Mushrooms'
Note that many lines below are examples of more than one technique. The examples given have been selected to avoid repetition.

Allusion
We shall by morning / Inherit the earth is an allusion to the Bible: *Blessed are the meek: for they shall inherit the earth.*

Assonance/internal rhyme
The 'I' and 'Y' sounds in the opening stanza

Overnight / very
Whitely, discreetly / Very quietly

Toes … noses … hold … loam fists insist etc.

Enjambment (run-on line)
our noses
Take hold on the loam

We
Diet on water

asking
Little or nothing

we are
Tables,

Imagery
Acquire the air

Shoulder through holes

Nudgers and shovers

Personification
Our toes, our noses / Take hold on the loam, / Acquire the air.

Soft fists insist on / Heaving the needles

Examples of critical vocabulary
1. B; 2. C; 3. B; 4. C; 5. A; 6. B; 7. B; 8. B; 9. B; 10. C; 11. B; 12. A; 13. A; 14. C; 15. B

More poetic terms
1. Sonnet; 2. Alliteration; 3. Limerick; 4. Onomatopoeia; 5. Metaphor; 6. Simile; 7. Personification; 8. Alliteration, Assonance; 9. Assonance; 10. Hyperbole; 11. Alliteration, Satire; 12. Personification and enjambment; 13. Alliteration; 14. Personification; 15. Rhyming couplet

She Dwelt Among the Untrodden Ways
1. B; 2. A; 3. A; 4. A; 5. C; 6. B; 7. A; 8. B; 9. B; 10. C

Drama

A.
1. C; 2. C; 3. B; 4. B; 5. C; 6. B; 7. C; 8. B; 9. A; 10. A

B.
1. Conflict; 2. Twist; 3. Narrative; 4. Contrast; 5. Contemporary; 6. Sub-plot; 7. Theatre; 8. Shakespearean; 9. Backdrop; 10. Stage directions

Film

1. C; 2. A; 3. A; 4. C; 5. A; 6. C; 7. C; 8. Performance; 9. Villain; 10. Credits; 11. Score; 12. Crescendo; 13. Composer; 14. Angle; 15. Close-up

Shakespearean Drama

1. C; 2. A; 3. B; 4. C; 5. C; 6. C; 7. B; 8. B; 9. B; 10. C

Novel and Short Story

1. C; 2. B; 3. B; 4. A; 5. B; 6. A; 7. A; 8. A; 9. C; 10. B

Narrative techniques

1. A; 2. B; 3. B; 4. B; 5. B; 6. B; 7. C; 8. A; 9. C; 10. A

Non-literary, Media and Visual Texts

Word	Definition
Homepage	The first page you see on a website, usually laying out the contents of the site
Documentary	A radio or TV programme using pictures /interviews/real events, to provide a factual report on a subject
Tagline	A catchphrase or slogan, often the words placed next to the logo on a webpage
Graphic novel	A novel in comic-strip format
Word cloud	A visual display of words used in a particular text or subject, in which the size of each word indicates its frequency or importance
Frame	A single picture in a comic strip
Blog	A regularly updated web page, often written by an individual or small group, in informal or conversational style
Tabloid	A compact size, popular newspaper, heavily illustrated with photographs and hyperbolic headlines, which prints sensational crime stories, short articles and celebrity gossip, often using hyperbole
VLE	A visual learning environment in which learning materials can be accessed online
Broadsheet	A large-format newspaper, with long articles, which prints serious news stories and uses a wider vocabulary than tabloids
Infographic	A diagram, often colourful, usually containing words and images, which lays out information in visual form
Audio text	A text designed for listening
Multi-modal text	A text which uses a variety of ways to communicate, e.g. spoken language, words, visuals, sounds, etc.
Vlog	A blog which includes video material
Navigation	How the user is helped to move from one page to another on a website

Self-evaluation for this section

Your scores in the tests tell you if you are on your way to achieving the relevant Learning Outcome.

Use an appropriate critical vocabulary when responding to literary texts.

As you progress in this examination book, you will advance your knowledge even further and fully achieve this Learning Outcome.

Here are my scores:

Test	Total mark	My marks
Critical terms	5 * 4 (20)	
General terms and vocabulary	15 * 2 (30)	
Poetry		
Examples of critical vocabulary	15 * 2 (30)	
Studied poetry quotations	15 * 6 (90)	
More poetic terms	15 * 2 (30)	
She Dwelt Among the Untrodden Ways	10 * 2 (20)	
Drama		
A. Multiple choice	10 * 2 (20)	
B. Complete the dramatic terms	10 * 2 (20)	
Film	15 * 2 (30)	
Shakespearean drama	10 * 2 (20)	
Novel and short story		
Multiple choice questions	10 * 2 (20)	
Narrative techniques	10 * 2 (20)	
Non-literary, media, digital	15 * 2 (30)	

The area(s) in which I scored worst was/were:

The area(s) in which I scored best was/were:

Here are two practical things I will do to improve my level of knowledge for the final examination:

1. ______________________________

2. ______________________________

Short Sample Questions

Appreciating Visual Genres: The Film Poster

Write a critical analysis of the poster for the film *The Glass Castle.*

In it, you should consider

- The visual impact of the poster

and

- Whether or not the poster makes you want to see the film.

The examiner will reward answers that are

- Clear
- Focused
- Well-expressed

The examiner will expect the best answers to

- Be grounded in the text (this means using evidence and quotation to support points).
- Include interesting, thoughtful ideas.
- Use the correct language for analysing a visual text.
- Be correct in points of grammar, punctuation and spelling.

The sample answer below

- Analyses a number of aspects of the poster for the film.
- Deals with each of the two bullet points.
- Develops and illustrates the points made with evidence and specific reference to the photograph.

The student has chosen to want to see the film.

Sample answer

This is an appealing, eye-catching, high-impact poster. It uses light, colour, landscape, character and atmosphere to attract an audience of all ages to the film. Having seen it, I would certainly want to see the story it about this family.

The happy image of a father, mother and three children suggests that this will be a family story. From the luggage piled on the roof, I guess they may be moving to a new home. I wonder what they've left behind? I notice that the children are close to the dad and the mother is on her own, so maybe they are distant from her? The battered, rusty old car and the old-fashioned clothes suggests a family short of money and a story set in the past. The car and the desert landscape look American.

Examiner's comment

Opening paragraph

Brief, clear opening sentence. Candidate uses correct terms. Responds to both elements in the question. Clear **focus** on the visual impact and what appeals to the candidate.

Second paragraph

Accurate description of characters, objects and setting.

The candidate is observant and can imagine a story from details in the poster. The candidate presents interesting **ideas** and an imaginative responses to the poster.

Although the landscape is barren, and it looks like the middle of nowhere, the bright, yellow light creates a joyful, optimistic atmosphere. Even if they are lost in a desert, this family looks cheerful, confident and hopeful for the future, wherever they are going. The facial expressions are bright and happy. The characters look lively, mom springing out of the car, smallest child perched on dad's shoulders. The older girl looks excited to be there. It seems as if they make an adventure of everything.

I like 'road films' where characters go searching for a new life, and I also like films set in the USA. Of the five characters in the picture I wonder whose story will be most important. I guess this is a film where the family grows up and maybe they're not always so united. I wonder what becomes of the girl with the old-fashioned dress and glasses. I wonder if the family stays together and if they live happily in their destination. Do they get to be better off? In conclusion, this is a high-impact poster because it catches an interesting moment, makes you curious and promises a good story.

Third paragraph
Strong on **development** of ideas and further analysis. Excellent references to large and small details in the image give **evidence** for ideas presented. **Creative, original ideas** show a thoughtful approach. Impressive **expression** and **vocabulary**, *mom springing … child perched.*

Final paragraph
Brings an interesting **personal response** to a **well-organised** answer. The candidate is imaginative and has thought deeply about the characters. He or she asks further thoughtful questions. Strong final sentence reinforces the points put forward in the answer as a whole.

Responding to Spoken Texts – Appreciating Language, Register and Audience

Sample 1 question

What elements of the manager's response make it **engaging** for listeners?
In your answer, you should make reference to **purpose**, **language**, **audience** and **impact**.

In the sample answer below:

- The key words from the question are **bold** in the answer.
- The answer is arranged in short paragraphs to pick up maximum marks.
- The first sentence in each paragraph is short and underlined.
- The candidate makes a **P**oint, **I**llustrates the point with evidence or quotation, and briefly **E**xplains the point in each paragraph.

Sample 1 answer

<u>The manager's **purpose** is to celebrate the achievement and engage the **audience** of listeners, players and supporters.</u> As manager, he must unite the fans and their team in in this victorious moment. He does three things that are very **engaging**. First, he analyses the performance; second, he pays tribute to everyone; third, he celebrates the victory.

He uses informal **language**, '*the lads worked their socks off*', complimenting the players and recognising the efforts of the losers, *'opposition, they kept knocking at the door'*. To maximise **impact** on his audience, he pays tribute to the fans and includes everyone who has supported the team.

Examiner's comment

Paragraph 1
Strong, clear first sentence states the purpose. The candidate addresses the key words in the question: *audience … engaging … language.*

Paragraph 2
Apt use of quotes to illustrate manager's informal language. Good expression, *pays tribute, victorious moment.*

His **language** is conversational. His audience like to hear familiar sporting phrases such as, *'knuckled down to it … bang on the game plan'*. His use of lively, dramatic **images** celebrates the big moments, *'took two sucker punches, laser-like kicks'*. He compliments the team's persistence and courage, and reminds supporters that this was a hard-won victory due to the team's persistence, *'backbone … didn't flinch … commitment, determination'*. His last sentence shows his understanding of his audience, 'we ain't goin' to flinch too handy'.

The impact is strong and positive, both for the team and the fans. The audience is engaged by his detailed, interesting, lively analysis of the game, the players are happy to hear what they had done well, and everyone is reminded of the best moments on the field.

Paragraph 3
Strong, clear first sentence about language. Good development and expansion. Notices imagery.

Good expression. Good vocabulary, *persistence hard-won victory*.

Excellent use of quotes to illustrate points.

Paragraph 4
Addresses impact, and audience.

Impressive three-point closing sentence sums up the answer.

Sample 2 question

Read this famous sentence from President John F. Kennedy's 1961 inauguration speech.

> Ask not what your country can do for you – ask what you can do for your country.

Analyse the statement using the following headings: **purpose**, **language**, **style**, **message**, **tone** and **impact**.

The examiner will be looking for a close analysis of this short text. Clear, focused, well-expressed answers that stick closely to the text and notice small details like punctuation and repetition will be rewarded.

Sample 2 answer

The **purpose** of an inauguration speech is to speak to the nation and to inspire admiration for, and confidence in, the new president. Although he uses simple, one-syllable words, the **language** is dignified and solemn, like the language of the Bible, *'Ask not …'*. The **style** is formal and elegant. This style is appropriate for a statesman who is marking a historic moment.

The **message** is that citizens should be unselfish, patriotic and noble. He challenges his audience to find ways to serve their country rather than asking *it* to serve *them*. The sentence breaks into two halves, with effective use of repetition in the word 'ask', and a clever internal rhyme, *'Ask not … ask what'*. It cleverly uses contrast. The negative first statement is balanced by the positive second part of the sentence. The pause made by the dash in the middle creates a big **impact**.

Examiner's comment

Paragraph 1
Strong, clear first sentence shows understanding of purpose.

Good description of language and style with quotation from and reference to the text. Excellent expression. The candidate has the vocabulary needed to describe language – *dignified, solemn, formal, elegant*.

Paragraph 2
Clear explanation of message. Candidate points out the use of contrast. Shows understanding of effective use of punctuation.

The mighty **impact** hits the listeners in the second half of the sentence. The **tone** is challenging, confident and strong with the emphasis on the word *you*, i.e. '*ask what* you *can do for your country*'.

Paragraph 3
Strong on impact and tone. Good use of quotation to illustrate points. Excellent closing sentence summarises points made.

Sample 3 question

Read the following extract from General Eisenhower's World War II speech, which was broadcast in June 1944 to 150,000 troops about to face the enemy on the Normandy beaches. Their mission was to liberate Europe from Nazi control.

In this speech, explain how the speaker shows understanding of his audience and uses language that suits his purpose.

Sample 3 answer

The president understands that he must lift the morale of his audience, the soldiers going into battle. He must inspire them to victory and let them know that their courage is appreciated both by him and by the nation. Therefore the language he uses is positive, inspiring, heroic and appreciative. I notice that his first words include all the armed forces, '*soldiers, sailors, airmen*'.

He shows understanding of the fears of his audience, going into battle against a powerful enemy. Therefore, he tells them that they are fighting for a great cause. Their aim is to achieve '*elimination of the Nazi tyranny*' and a '*free world*'. He is also realistic. He says he understands that the enemy will '*fight savagely*'. His speech must inspire courage, so he builds morale by telling them '*the tide has turned*' and they are '*marching together to Victory!*'

His language suits his heroic purpose. He uses solemn, ancient words that make this mission sound important and historic, e.g. '*embark … Great Crusade … brothers in arms*'. He tells them that '*the eyes of the world are upon*' them. In contrast with the negative language about the enemy, '*destruction … tyranny*', all the language about the Allies is positive, '*great reserves … prayers … security … free men.*' I like the alliteration in '*liberty-loving*'. The language builds up to a climax in the dramatic phrases of the final lines where he tells them that he believes in their '*courage and devotion*'. The speech ends with a dramatic exclamation mark, '*nothing less than full Victory!*'

Examiner's comment

Paragraph 1
The first sentence gives a clear statement of the speaker's understanding of his audience and purpose. Ambitious vocabulary used to describe language in the text, *positive*, *inspiring*, *heroic*, *appreciative*.

Paragraph 2
Strong, clear opening statement deals with understanding the feelings of the listeners to this speech. Good ideas and development of points with evidence and quotations from the text. The point made in the leader sentence is both well developed and backed up with accurate quotation.

Paragraph 3
Good development of both language and purpose. Excellent vocabulary to describe the language, *solemn*, *ancient words*. Points out positive and negative language in the speech. Well-spotted alliteration. The student has noticed the effective use of punctuation, i.e. the exclamation mark to create dramatic effect. The student has caught the tone of the speech.

Reading to Analyse and Evaluate

Explain what aspects of this press release would attract listeners to the programme *Pull Like a Dog*. Refer to aspects of the text to support your response.

Tip

Notice that this answer is well organised in three short paragraphs. Each paragraph makes points about different aspects.

Sample answer

The first **aspect of the text that would attract listeners** is the **clever, attention-catching title**, *Pull Like a Dog*. This title is funny but it also shows the determination of these rowers. The producers say that this is a 'special' documentary, so something extraordinary is promised. Success is emphasised by the Olympic medal in the first sentence. The photograph showing the dynamic, smiling brothers is also eye-catching.

The **words and phrases are carefully chosen** to **attract** an audience who want to hear a happy, exciting story. Phrases like *'came from nowhere'* and *'bolting their way'* are dramatic. Their amazing successes are trumpeted in phrases like *'the first ever'* and *'the fastest singles lightweight rower on the planet'*. Listeners will want to find out how two young men came from nowhere to be the world's famous best.

Their **likeable personalities**, revealed both in the phrases and in the photograph would **attract** a wide audience of all ages to the programme. Their funny catchphrases like 'Steak and spuds' made people laugh. They come from a small parish. Their small club is now 'the most successful club in Irish rowing history'. Everyone loves a story about the ordinary person shooting to fame. Young, ambitious athletes will like hearing that small parishes with small clubs can produce great athletes.

Examiner's comment

Paragraph 1

Thoughtful analysis of the title. Uses the words of the question in the opening sentence. Good expression and vocabulary, *something extraordinary is promised … dynamic … eye-catching.* Excellent opening sentence with clear focus on the question. The point made in the opening sentence is well developed in the rest of the paragraph.

Paragraph 2

Analysis of vocabulary: uses evidence of particular words and phrases to illustrate the point. Appreciation and understanding of register. Good vocabulary, *amazing successes are trumpeted*. Understanding of audience response.

Paragraph 3

Further development of high-quality ideas. Shows appreciation of humorous language. Points out appeal to different age groups. Strong, well-expressed closing sentence.

Reading for Comparison

Comparing the final words in films

Choose the ending you think would have the greater impact on a cinema audience and give reasons for your choice:

a. *I do wish we could chat longer, but … I'm having an old friend for dinner. Bye.*

b. *If you strike me down, I shall become more powerful than you can possibly imagine.*

Sample answer

I think the menacing words spoken by the serial killer would have the greater impact because there is an evil humour in these words. I imagine a soft, but menacing tone of voice, grinning slyly at the double meaning in 'having an old friend for dinner', and then pausing for a moment before chirping a cheery 'Bye', which would make the audience smile and then shudder at how evil he sounds.

His words seem courteous, friendly and old-fashioned, 'I do wish we could chat longer', as if he is a humble, harmless old gentleman. Actually, he is gloating that he has outwitted everyone and is planning his next killing. He is enjoying sniggering at the agent, creating terror and boasting about his next murder.

In the little pause before 'Bye' he is probably waiting for the full impact of his words to sink in and smiling to himself. The impact is terrifying. The audience may smile for a moment at the pun, but then the true meaning dawns on them and they imagine that another gruesome murder will happen that evening. The final feeling for the audience is terror. The emotions of the film continue as the lights come on and they leave the cinema.

Examiner's comment

Paragraph 1

Opening sentence makes a clear statement of choice, using the words of the question and giving a thoughtful reason for the choice.

Explanation of the double meaning. Excellent description of the actor's tone of voice. Well expressed with good vocabulary.

Paragraph 2

Insight into character of the speaker. Excellent expression. Good ideas and development of points made.

The candidate explains what the words reveal about the character and about the story.

Paragraph 3

Excellent description of the impact on the audience. Shows understanding of the term 'pun'. Strong closing sentence shows imagination and appreciation of the closing words.

Now it's your turn ...

Now you write the answer, choosing Obi-Wan's words as those having the greater impact: *If you strike me down, I shall become more powerful than you can possibly imagine.*

Comparing novel openings

Compare and contrast.

- Identify **one technique** that is used by **both** writers to try to 'hook' the reader.
- Point out one **different** technique used by **one** of the writers to try to capture the reader's attention and create interest in the story.

Sample answer

Each of these openings captures attention, excites the imagination and makes the reader curious to continue reading. The 'hook' used by both writers is the striking, stand-alone opening sentence. In each case, it stands alone at the top of the paragraph, surprising the reader with a startling statement. In different ways, each sentence says that something terrible has happened. Then there is a pause before the story begins.

'When the doorbell rings at three in the morning, it's never good news' sounds dark and ominous. *'On the day Emma Carstair's parents were killed, the weather*

Examiner's comment

Paragraph 1

The opening responds clearly and strongly to the statement for discussion, using the key words and phrases in the question. The candidate points out the striking technique of the stand-alone sentence and the pause before the narrative begins.

Thoughtful, interesting comment on each of the opening sentences.

was perfect' is a strange statement because a report of a murder does not usually mention the weather.

Anthony Horowitz captures the reader's attention by creating suspense. He builds up tension by precisely describing small details. You picture the character lying still in the bed, hearing the first chime of the doorbell, then the creak of the stair, the second chime and the rattle of the security chain. He creates an eerie atmosphere with the glow of the clock in the dark. The reader is waiting for the bad news, remembering the chapter title, 'Funeral Voices'.

Paragraph 3
Excellent analysis of the technique of creating an atmosphere of suspense in the second text. Thoughtful observation on the chapter title.

Responding to Texts – Appreciating Language, Story and Action

Ptolemy's Gate extract

In the opening paragraph, point out:

A.

1. Two examples of alliteration

   four fleet; a cheetah on a chain

2. Three examples of a good choice of verb

   dropped; crouched; sniffing; stole; stirred; cried

3. The noun that tells you a murder is planned

   assassins

4. Two examples of sound images

   the pattering of rain; jackals cried

5. One example of a dramatic visual image

   The assassins dropped into the palace grounds at midnight, four fleet shadows dark against the wall; they crouched there, low and motionless, sniffing at the air; the dark gardens; a cheetah on a chain stirred in its sleep; jackals cried

6. Two details that give you a strong sense of the setting

   the palace grounds at midnight; the tamarisks and date palms; a cheetah on a chain; jackals cried

B.

Explain in your own words what is happening in this opening scene.

The year is 125 BC. Four assassins climb over the walls of a palace in Alexandria. They crouch silently in the grass for a few seconds. In the cold moonlight, they move stealthily towards the quarters of their victim, a boy, sleeping on the first floor, who is guarded by a cheetah. The royal guards are playing cards and the servants are asleep as the assassins begin to climb.

C.

Write a promotional press release for this novel, telling readers that the first page will grip them. Base your writing only on the extract.

Sample answer

Jonathan Stroud's latest novel does not disappoint, particularly in its gripping opening scene. In the first paragraph, we are transported to long ago and far away, i.e. Alexandria in 125 BC. With the single word 'assassins', the opening sentence reveals a murder attempt. The intended victim is a boy, sleeping in a palace and guarded by a cheetah. Supernatural spirits and an exotic **setting** in Alexandria form the backdrop for this opening scene.

Jonathan Stroud creates **suspense** with his wonderful storytelling skills. The descriptions of four murderers, '*on pointed toe-tips*', moving silently through palace gardens is gripping. Ominous **images** such as '*black shadows*' and '*secret as a scorpion*', **foreshadow** the murder attempt. In a touch of **irony**, we are told that the palace gates, bypassed by the assassins, are *locked by triple bolts*.

Jonathan Stroud is a master of storytelling and his writing is **poetic**. We find **alliteration** in '*cheetah on a chain*', and **personification** in '*death came calling*'. As the assassins begin to climb to the bedroom, '*suspended by their fingertips and the nails of their big toes*', the reader's imagination is sparked. What **twist** might come? The first page will grip you and you will want to read on and enjoy more of the exciting **plot**.

Examiner's comment

Paragraph 1

Strong, clear opening sentence directly addresses the question. The candidate appreciates the novelist's skill in creating a setting. Shows understanding and appreciation of language with quotation from the text, 'assassins'. This introduction shows attention to detail in the text.

Paragraph 2

Candidate uses appropriate terminology for fiction. Points re storytelling, suspense, imagery and irony are well developed.

Paragraph 3

Strong summary of a well-organised answer. Creative ideas re poetic language and excellent use of evidence and quotation. Use of key words from the question.

Responding to the Special Language of Poetry

The title of the poem is 'Mushrooms'. In your opinion, is it only about mushrooms or might it tell another story? Write your interpretation of the poem, justifying your opinion with quotations from the text.

Sample answer which uses PIE

In my opinion, this poem is about slaves who are planning a revolution against their masters. The slaves' plan is to rise up in the middle of the night, like silent ghosts, '*Overnight, very / Whitely*', sneaking up from the underground, suffocating cellars where they are forced to '*sleep*'. All are loyal to the cause, '*Nobody … betrays us*'.

Tip

This answer makes a **Point** at the beginning of each paragraph, then **Illustrates** it and **Explains** it.

They will strike with all their might even if they have to suffer pain, '*Heaving the needles*'. They are badly fed, '*Diet on water*', so they are used to hardship. They will become a massive army, '*So many of us*!' who will surprise, attack and defeat.

They are disciplined, courageous and persistent. Although progress is slow and the journey is tough, they keep pressing on like a well trained army, silently but relentlessly, taking hold, heaving and shouldering their way through little cracks.

The masters have been so cruel that they think the slaves are beaten down, *'we are meek'*. But the slaves will advance and get others to join them, *'Our kind multiplies'*. They are planners and smart strategists.

They are clever strategists, always pushing forward slowly but with determination, 'Nudgers and shovers'.

Reading Comprehension Strategies

Commentary on the NASA homepage

Sample answer

Teachers and members of the Student Council,

I show you this NASA homepage as a fine example of a well-designed website. I believe it can serve as a model for us on how to lay out our website; what we should include; and how we will use the homepage to attract parents and students from the local primary schools.

You will notice the NASA **logo** thoughtfully placed in the top left corner where it catches your eye. We can do likewise with our school crest and our school motto.

The NASA **header** goes from *Missions* through *Galleries* and *About* to *NASA Audiences*. We can substitute our *Gallery* of photographs and *News, About Us*, etc.

We have an interesting selection of **links** to place in the **Navigation pane**, e.g. our extra-curricular activities, the subjects we do and the clubs you can join. We should also place our **social links**, i.e. our Twitter and Facebook pages, here.

Like NASA, we can place **events** and our school **calendar** on the homepage so that parents can see that we have a lot going on. We should have a special spot for **latest news**.

The white piece of text could be a selection of real comments from students in the school saying why they came here and what they like about life in our school.

This design is very strong on **colour** and **visual images**, which we can do also with a background screen of our school building and playing fields. I suggest an autumn scene when the trees look colourful. Where they have one photograph of a star astronaut, we can place two photographs of students, one showing prize-winners in the Young Scientist and Technology Exhibition, in sport or in debating; the other a scene from an ordinary day

Examiner's comment

The student correctly addresses the audience.

Language and style are appropriate for a formal address to an audience of teachers and the Student Council.

This answer shows good knowledge of the correct terms for website design.

Also shows understanding of the importance of layout, colour and other elements.

The presentation is efficiently organised in sections on different aspects of the website.

There are creative, original ideas such as students' comments on school life.

The closing paragraph presents a point about colour and visual images and then goes on to develop that point with illustrations and suggestions.

in the life of the school, e.g. students playing music or in class. The photographs should be placed on a dark background to make them stand out.

Responding to Shakespeare

Hamlet

Here is Polonius's advice in modern English:

Don't blurt out everything you're thinking. Keep your opinions to yourself and don't rush into action before thinking things through. Be loyal and faithful to your old friends and don't be hasty in making friends with new people you don't know. Steer clear of fights, but once you're in a fight, be ruthless. If you have to fight, make sure you win. Take in other people's opinions but know your own mind. Do more listening than talking. Buy the best clothes you can afford, but no showing off. You are what you wear. The best people in France have very good taste in clothes. Don't lend money and don't borrow either. Manage your money carefully. Be true to yourself and you won't go wrong.

A.

1. *And these few precepts in thy memory / See thou character; 2. C; 3. Give thy thoughts no tongue; 4. Give every man thy ear, but few thy voice; 5. A; 6. C; 7. B; 8. C; 9. B; 10. For loan oft loses both itself and friend*

B.

Explain **two** imaginative things a director could do to stage this long speech from the play.

The speech begins with Polonius telling his son to hurry up because,

The wind sits in the shoulder of your sail.

Firstly, I would create an imaginative setting on stage with bright lighting and dramatic sound effects. A wind machine to the side of the stage would billow two very large white sails, so they would flap loudly in the wind. The lighting effects would make shadows of flapping seagulls and the sound effects would roar their squawking. The sound of crashing waves would suggest a storm blowing up. These sights and sounds would make the speech sound urgent and important, as if Polonius is calming his nerves before his son sets off on a dangerous sea voyage.

Secondly, I would place father and son centre stage and a girl upstage. She could be Laertes' girlfriend or sister. As Polonius is giving all this advice, which Laertes is only half listening to, he could be smiling at the girl. If she is his sister, they have heard all this before. If she is his girlfriend, he is more interested in her than in what his dad is saying. He has his foot on the gangplank and he is

Examiner's comment

Focus: The opening sentence mentions two aspects of imaginative staging, i.e. lighting and sound effects. Excellent grounding of the setting in the words of the speech. Good linking of sound effects with Polonius's fears for his son's safety.

Ideas: The candidate demonstrates knowledge of stagecraft terms and creative ideas in staging. Ideas are supported by evidence and details from the speech and the characters involved. Candidate pays attention to **tone** and **gesture** in dialogue, e.g. Laertes smiling and attempting to move and Polonius tugging at his sleeve.

looking round at the girl behind them most of the time. Every few lines, he should turn to the ship and start up the gangplank, but Polonius keeps tugging at his sleeve and giving more unwanted advice.

When he says,

Costly thy habit as thy purse can buy

he should point at the clothes Laertes is wearing because he has bought him new clothes for his new life at university.

When he says,

This above all: to thine own self be true,

he should gently put his hand on his son's shoulder as if this is the most important thing he has to say. I would direct Laertes to look straight at Polonius as if this is the one thing he is taking notice of.

Organisation: The ideas are clearly organised in separate paragraphs. The **second** point is clearly stated, developed and illustrated in the second paragraph. The third paragraph makes good use of quotation from the text.

Language: Very good expression and extensive vocabulary, especially in the use of a wide variety of verbs, *billow ... flapping ... tugging*

Careful attention is paid to grammar, spelling and punctuation throughout the answer.

Self-evaluation

Read over ***your*** answer and give yourself an assessment using the grid on the next page.

Remember the success criteria for **FIDOL**:

Focus: You answered the question you were asked, in full, not leaving out any parts. You demonstrated strong, clear **focus** on the key words in the question from beginning to end. You remembered to make reference to the word *imaginative*.

Ideas: You presented creative, imaginative, interesting, thoughtful **ideas** that showed you had thought deeply about the question and clearly imagined the stage, the setting and the voice, movement and gestures of the characters.

Development: When you made a point, you went on to **develop** and back it up with evidence and/or quotation from the speech. Your quotations were accurate.

Organisation: You kept answering the question you were asked. Your answer was presented in a series of short paragraphs, each having a separate point. Your answer began with an introduction and finished with a conclusion.

Language: Your grammar and spelling were correct. You put punctuation marks where they were needed. Your expression and your vocabulary were both good.

Total 20 marks for each category	High (20–19)	Medium (18–12)	Low (11–0)	If the answer was not in the high category, what could you do to improve?
Focus				
Ideas				
Development				
Organisation				
Language				

Richard III

1. Match the character to the description.

The character who is speaking the soliloquy	A. Richard
Richard's older brother, who is in line to become king on the death of the present king	C. Clarence
The King of England as the play begins	B. Edward

2. Write the words from the speech that match the modern English.

Our dark, unhappy time has been changed to sunshine days	Now is the winter of our discontent Made glorious summer
Dark-faced war	Grim-visag'd war
Instead of climbing on to armed horses	instead of mounting barbed steeds
To frighten terrifying enemies	To fright the souls of fearful adversaries
A word that means *smartly*, *quickly*	nimbly
A woman's bedroom	a lady's chamber
I was not created athletic and sporty	But I, that am not shap'd for sportive tricks
Ugly, badly made, premature and small when I was born into this world	Deform'd, unfinish'd, sent before my time Into this breathing world
I have decided to be evil	I am determined to prove a villain
Time to hide what I'm thinking; here comes Clarence	Dive, thoughts, down to my soul, here Clarence comes

3. If you were the actor playing Richard on stage, explain how you would keep the audience interested throughout this long opening speech. In your answer, you may refer to your voice, your gestures, props, where you would stand, sit or walk etc.

Self-evaluation

Read over your answer and give yourself an assessment using the following grid.

Remember the success criteria for FIDOL:

Focus: You answered the question you were asked, in full, not leaving out any parts. You demonstrated strong, clear **focus** on the key words in the question from beginning to end.

Ideas: You presented creative, imaginative, interesting, thoughtful **ideas** that showed you had thought deeply about the question and clearly imagined the stage, the setting and the voice, movement and gestures of the actor.

Development: When you made a point, you went on to **develop** the point and back it up with evidence and/or quotation from the speech. Your quotations were accurate.

Organisation: You kept answering the question you were asked. Your answer was presented in a series of short paragraphs, each having a separate point. Your answer began with an introduction and finished with a conclusion.

Language: Your grammar and spelling were correct. You put punctuation marks where they were needed. Your expression and your vocabulary were both good.

Total 20 marks for each category	High (20–19)	Medium (18–12)	Low (11–0)	If the answer was not in the high category, what could you do to improve?
Focus				
Ideas				
Development				
Organisation				
Language				

Self-evaluation for this section

You should by now have made progress in understanding Shakespeare's language.

Record your scores out of 20 for the extracts in this section:

Play extract	**My score out of 20 was ...**
Hamlet Polonius to his son, Laertes	
Richard III Richard's opening speech	

Look back at how you assessed your paragraphed answers, using FIDOL.

Estimate your strongest areas. Which areas do you need to improve on?

	Focus	**Ideas**	**Development**	**Organisation**	**Language**
Hamlet					
Richard III					

Conclusion:

I am strongest in these areas: ______________________________

____

I need to improve my answers in this/these area(s):

____

____

Here are three key scenes from my studied Shakespeare that I am going to revise, and from which I will learn a set of accurate quotations:

1. ______________________________

2. ______________________________

3. ______________________________

Write for a Variety of Purposes

Write Descriptively

Scrooge's meeting with the ghost of Jacob Marley

This is just *one* sample of possible words. You will find many more **adjectives and verbs to use in your descriptive writing**.

It is Christmas Eve and an icy wind blows through London. Hard-hearted, tight-fisted Scrooge is dozing by a tiny fire in his gloomy sitting room. Suddenly, he hears the sound of the cellar door crashing open. A clanking noise, like someone dragging a chain across a wooden floor, booms through the house. The sound of slow footsteps approaches him and he trembles with fear.

He turns abruptly to see the terrifying face of Jacob Marley, with its death-cold eyes, laden down with heavy chains, padlocks and cash boxes.

Who are you?

In life, I was your partner, Jacob Marley.

Write to Create Tension or Suspense

A character attempts to escape

Sample 1 – this student has chosen her words carefully to show the examiner that she has the vocabulary needed to create suspense.

Tallulah Rockefeller had waited **patiently** for her **captor** to fall asleep before she wriggled **noiselessly through** the **tiny** window. **Dropping silently** to the pavement below, she **sprinted** through the **dark** alley, **panting, stumbling, clambering wildly** over heaps of **stinking** bin-bags and **shattered** bottles. She could hear her **pounding** heart. **Boom, boom, boom** it went as if it might **explode** at any moment. Her throat was on fire, but she knew she must make ground before they discovered she had fled. *Don't stop, keep running, if you fall you're finished*, she told herself.

Sample 2 – this student has imagined a different scenario.

In the dawn light, the thin figure **slipped softly** and **silently** out of the apartment, **glancing nervously** up the **deserted** street to check for unfamiliar vehicles or **watching eyes**. Two days ago, he had **fled** from the secret police massacre in the town square. Soon, they would come to arrest him and he would become another of the 'disappeared'. His **grim** face and **sad eyes** showed that he had not dared to say *goodbye*. Better that his family know nothing. He would flee the dangers of the city on the early train which could take him across the border to safety. At the entrance to the railway station, an **unmarked black car** sat at the kerbside, with a view over all approaches. The **silent men** inside watched and waited.

Key Vocabulary for the Examination

A.

1. Texts; 2. Extract; 3. Passage; 4. Setting; 5. Analyse; 6. Narrator; 7. Register; 8. Impact; 9. Engaging; 10. Dialogue; 11. Effective; 12. Structure; 13. Irrelevant; 14. Striking; 15. Gist

B.

1. Technique; 2. Caption; 3. Author; 4. Prose; 5. Infographic; 6. Contrasting; 7. Analyse; 8. Communicate; 9. Aspects; 10. Accurate; 11. Qualities; 12. Justify; 13. Context; 14. Adapted; 15. Significant

Sample Paper 1 – Journeys

Section A

Question 1

From your reading of this script, point out some of the imaginative ways in which this radio documentary tells a story and engages the radio audience.

Possible points for this answer:

- Use of sound effects
- The voice of a narrator to tell the story
- The story moves between past and present
- The first words spoken are the time and the place
- Characters telling their own story, remembering the past
- Different voices with different registers
- Radio archive (news broadcast from 1985)
- Music to create atmosphere or link with the theme
- Interesting title that makes listeners curious about the story to follow

Sample answer

This radio documentary **tells its story of an amazing journey using many techniques** to **engage listeners**: an interesting introduction; sound effects; the ordinary voice of Keith and the formal voice of narrator and newsreader; and research from the past. These techniques **tell the story** dramatically and also **catch and hold the attention** of the radio audience.

The short introduction promises an interesting story, making listeners curious about how two boys 'bunked' from Darndale as far as New York. In the opening moments, the dramatic sound effects of beeping alarms and wheels on tracks catch listeners' attention, *FX: … train door beeping alarm.* These sounds create atmosphere, helping radio listeners to visualise the story as the journey moves on to the new sound of the *Ferry boat horn*. The song about *the lost weekend* is clever and appealing.

In my opinion, the most engaging thing of all is the voice of Keith telling his story in his own words, '*so these were all kind of new places … we'd go over to bunk on the ferry over to England*'. The story is told more formally by the narrator, who says '*they could now venture far afield from their home to an epic journey that will become front page news*'.

Examiner's comment

Paragraph 1

Clear introduction. Candidate names four different techniques. Strong focus on the key words in the question.

Paragraph 2

Excellent introductory sentence. Good development of points re. the use of sound effects to dramatise a radio documentary.

Paragraph 3

Strong opening sentence. Point about different formal and informal voices is well developed in the paragraph.

Excellent use of accurate quotations to illustrate ideas and back up points made.

Documentary also uses research to bring in voices from the past. The 1985 newsreader says, '*Two Dublin boys, aged 10 and 13, have been returned to Ireland after stowing away*'. The use of varied techniques to tell the story and engage listeners makes for an interesting and enjoyable documentary.

Paragraph 4
Clear point regarding the use of research in radio documentary.

Strong closing sentence.

Every point made is supported by quotation or evidence from the text. Spelling, grammar and punctuation are correct throughout.

Question 2
From your reading of the introduction and the extract, what elements of this story do you think would be appealing to a radio audience?

Possible points for this answer:

- A home story about young Irish boys
- curiosity about how they got through airport security
- Interest in airport security nowadays
- People remembering things from their own childhood
- Sounds like a story that would make you laugh
- The amazing nature of the journey
- The appeal of an adult looking back to his youth
- Appeal to different age groups of listeners
- A front page news story about ordinary people
- The different voices telling the story from different points of view
- The voice of Keith talking about 'adventure'
- The voice of the narrator in the background
- The sound effects to make it all seem real
- A story that sounds impossible but really happened
- Listeners love a story about an unusual journey

Imagine you are the examiner.
Read your answer carefully.
Judge it as high, medium or low, according to the headings in the rows below.
Justify the box you ticked in each case.
If you placed the answer in the medium category, explain what change would move it up to high.
If you placed the answer in the low category, explain what change would move it up to medium.

	High	Medium	Low	Say what change(s) would move this aspect of the answer up to a higher category.
Clear opening statement that addresses the question				
Answers fully the question that was asked, uses key words from the question				
Good ideas, creative, interesting to read				
Ideas are stated and then well developed				
Good use of reference or quotation from the text to illustrate and support the points that are made				
Organised piece of writing with good paragraphing				
Ideas are well expressed, good vocabulary				
Strong closing sentence				
Spelling, punctuation and grammar are at a high standard throughout				

Question 3

Write a critical analysis of this photograph, explaining how you think it adds to the impact of the newspaper headline.

Possible points for this answer:

- Highlighting the hardship and sadness of the situation
- Composition and layout
- Light, colour, shadows
- Contrast
- It gives a human face to the statistic
- It shows children playing
- Foreground and background
- Mother and children in the frame
- Facial expressions
- Emotions expressed by the images

Sample answer

This photograph shows refugees from the city of Mosul, who have left their homes to live in a refugee camp. The photograph has been carefully composed in different sections so that it succeeds in its aim to send a message to the world. In the foreground is a woman with two small children. In the background are two men, another woman and some children playing on a makeshift swing. The ground is rough, and the background shows a sea of white tents.

The photograph gives a human face to the statistic of one million people in the headlines. The human message is clear. This image shows readers that families have lost their homes and now live on rough ground cramped together in tents. The mother's facial expression is tense and worried. Dark shadows fall on the tents in the background. The children don't understand that there is a war and find a way to play like little children anywhere in the world.

The colours are few and strong. We see black, white and different shades of red or pink. The impact is very strong, because everything frames just three of the '*One million*' people who have had to '*flee Mosul*' and make a desperate journey.

Examiner's comment

Paragraph 1

Clear focus. The candidate states clearly who and what the photograph shows. Refers to careful composition, describes foreground and background.

High quality ideas and observations.

Uses detail from the poster to illustrate ideas.

Paragraph 2

Clear opening sentence. Points are supported by quotation or evidence from the text. Shows understanding of humanitarian message. Develops ideas about the message of the photograph.

Paragraph 3

Clearly expressed summary with focus on the key words in the question. Strong closing sentence.

Section B

Question 4

(a) B; (b) B; (c) C; (d) A; (e) B

Question 5

Choose **two** of the seven ages described by Jaques.

In the case of each choice, describe how you think the actor might use voice, facial expression, a dramatic gesture or movement and/or a prop in order to perform this speech in an imaginative way.

Sample answer

This candidate chose **age 3,** the soldier, and **age 7**, the elderly man in the last stage of life.

The answer begins with a general statement about the need for props for each of the seven stages.

The actor should have many props and should use voice, facial expression, gesture and movement to keep the attention of the audience in this long speech. I have chosen the soldier and the elderly man. I will describe their voices, facial expressions, small gestures and movements, and the props that would help them perform this speech in an imaginative way.

Examiner's comment

Paragraph 1

Clear focus on the question in the opening sentence. Candidate states how the question will be addressed using key words from the question.

To play the part of the soldier, the actor should raise his voice loudly and proudly to show his vanity in being young, strong and brave. He should stroke his beard, and smile proudly because he wants people to think he is stylish and good looking. I imagine him suddenly surprising the audience by swooping down and grabbing a sword from the floor in a big show-off gesture. Then he should point it dramatically at the audience, like a performing swordsman. The word '*reputation*' should be spoken slowly and sarcastically, because the actor knows that it is as fragile as a bubble.

Paragraph 2
Clear opening sentence. Points are supported by quotation or evidence from the text. Attention is paid to voice, facial expression, gesture and movement . Creative suggestion for prop. Impressive expression and vocabulary, *swooping down ... performing swordsman*. Strong points are made about the actor's tone of voice and meaning of the lines.

For the '*last*' age, the actor needs to look and sound frail and tired. He should stoop his back so he looks small and maybe in pain from arthritis. As he speaks, he should shuffle slowly as if he is in slippers. His prop is a pair of spectacles which he fumbles with and settles on his nose with a slow, clumsy gesture. His once '*manly*' voice is fading to a whisper, so the actor should speak hoarsely, in a little, thin squeak.

Paragraph 3
Strong opening sentence which is developed through the paragraph. Attention is paid to voice, facial expression, gesture and movement. Creative suggestion for prop and gestures to accompany it.

Strong closing sentence with good use of single word quotation.

Section C

Question 8
Poem ***The General***

Identify a line or lines in the poem where the poet uses each of the following poetic techniques.

1. Rhyming couplet

   'He's a cheery old card,' grunted Harry to Jack
   As they slogged up to Arras with rifle and pack

2. Assonance

   *'He's **a** cheery old c**a**rd,' grunted H**a**rry to J**a**ck*

3. Alliteration

   ***l**ast **w**eek on our **w**ay to the **l**ine*

4. Effective use of pause

   ... with rifle and pack.

   But he did for them both with his plan of attack.

Section D

Question 10

(a) The Central Statistics Office (or CSO)

(b) 25%

(c) True – urban populations are growing faster that rural populations.

(d) True – only 40% of the population lives within 5 km of the coast. Therefore 60% live more than 5 km from the coast.

(e) False – Saggart has had an increase of 46.1%.

Question 11

(a) quiet / quite

(b) seen / scene

(c) bawl / ball

(d) their / there

(e) whether / weather

Sample Paper 2 – Persuasion

Section A

Question 1

(a) B; (b) A; (c) C; (d) B; (e) C.

Question 2

Select one character from a Shakespearean play you have studied and list five adjectives that describe this character.

Expand your store of **adjectives** to describe dramatic characters.

Romeo and Juliet

There are more than 20 named characters in the play. You can choose any one of them.

On the next page, you will find many examples of adjectives to help you.

Remember!

When making a list of adjectives, you can use **synonyms** (words that have the same meaning), e.g.:

The nurse is **talkative** – chatty, garrulous, gossipy …

Cassius is **cunning** – shrewd, clever, manipulative, calculating, crafty, unscrupulous, sly, wily, devious …

Use your dictionary or thesaurus for any adjectives you don't understand.

If this is your studied play, add another adjective of your own in each case.

Also, add another character in the blank box.

The nurse
1. Warm-hearted
2. Talkative
3. Motherly
4. Caring
5. Vulgar
6. ____________________

Romeo
1. Impulsive
2. Romantic
3. Passionate
4. Courageous
5. Rash
6. ____________________

Tybalt
1. Aggressive
2. Short-tempered
3. Macho
4. Proud
5. Immature
6. ____________________

Juliet
1. Quiet
2. Innocent
3. Passionate
4. Independent
5. Courageous
6. ____________________

Capulet
1. Traditional
2. Generous
3. Sociable
4. Stern
5. Volatile
6. ____________________

____
1. ____________________
2. ____________________
3. ____________________
4. ____________________
5. ____________________

Julius Caesar

If this is your studied play, add another adjective of your own in each case.

Also, add another character in the blank box.

Julius Caesar
1. Proud
2. Arrogant
3. Powerful
4. Flawed
5. Respected
6. ____________________

Brutus
1. Traditional
2. Noble
3. Naive
4. Honest
5. Respected
6. ____________________

Cassius
1. Ambitious
2. Shrewd
3. Manipulative
4. Ruthless
5. Cunning
6. ____________________

____
1. ____________________
2. ____________________
3. ____________________
4. ____________________
5. ____________________

Henry IV Part 1

If this is your studied play, add another adjective of your own in each case.

Also, add another character in the blank box.

Prince Hal	**Falstaff**	**Hotspur**	
1. Wayward	1. Drunken	1. Quick-tempered	______________
2. Wild	2. Lazy	2. Brave	1. ____________
3. Royal	3. Funny	3. Ambitious	2. ____________
4. Intelligent	4. Fat	4. Honourable	3. ____________
5. Brave	5. Talkative	5. Heroic	4. ____________
6. ____________	6. ____________	6. ____________	5. ____________

The Merchant of Venice

If this is your studied play, add another adjective of your own in each case.

Also, add another character in the blank box.

Shylock	**Antonio**	**Portia**	
1. Shrewd	1. Rich	1. Confident	______________
2. Vengeful	2. Successful	2. Beautiful	1. ____________
3. Persecuted	3. Depressed	3. Rich	2. ____________
4. Humiliated	4. Sad	4. Witty	3. ____________
5. Excluded	5. Generous	5. Clever	4. ____________
6. ____________	6. ____________	6. ____________	5. ____________

A Midsummer Night's Dream

If this is your studied play, add another adjective of your own in each case.

Also, add another character in the blank box.

Hermia	**Demetrius**	**Puck**	
1. Independent	1. Arrogant	1. Mischievous	______________
2. Fiery	2. Stubborn	2. Magic	1. ____________
3. Daring	3. Unpredictable	3. Supernatural	2. ____________
4. Disobedient	4. Determined	4. Clever	3. ____________
5. Strong	5. Romantic	5. Funny	4. ____________
6. ____________	6. ____________	6. ____________	5. ____________

Question 3

Write a critical analysis of the poster of the BBC's film version of ***Henry V***.

In your analysis you should consider:

- The visual impact of the poster

and

- Whether or not the poster makes you want to see the film.

Possible points:

- Colour
- Background and foreground details
- Areas of light/darkness
- Military horses and harness
- Characters/position of the characters
- Warrior king
- White horse
- Costume
- Facial expressions
- The appeal of the characters
- The promise of a story in the visual images
- Other details in the poster
- Dramatic impact etc.

Sample answer

In my opinion, this poster makes a powerful visual impact due to its visual techniques. These include light and colour, costume, character and contrast. This strong visual impact, with its attractive use of strong military horses and strong leader and warriors promises dramatic action and would make me want to see the film. The light blue sky in the background sets off the characters in the foreground.

I notice a small number of colours, black, blue, brown and the golden crown, which create strong visual impact. There are contrasting bright and dark areas. There is dramatic impact in the different colours of the horses, the shining chain mail, leather harness to protect the horses in battle and the dark military costumes.

The grey fortress or castle to the side emphasises the idea of a war story. Bright light shines on the dazzling, handsome warrior king who is at the front, on a white steed, followed by loyal men on brown or black horses. The luminous background makes him the heroic knight in shining armour. He is dressed in steely battle armour, ready for a courageous fight on the battlefield. This presents him as a soldier king ready to conquer the enemy. His facial expression is strong and determined, as are the grim and determined facial expressions of his followers on horseback behind him.

Examiner's comment

The **opening paragraph** states a clear focus on each part of the question and lays out the techniques that the candidate will discuss. The candidate uses the correct terminology for a visual image.

Paragraph 2
Good development of contrast in the poster. Original, creative ideas. Good observations of details. Clear focus on characters, horses, colours and costume.

Paragraph 3
The candidate develops contrasts and has noticed positions, effective use of lighting, facial expressions and has the vocabulary to describe them. Excellent expression, *Bright light shines on the dazzling ... white steed*. Interesting observations on the facial expressions in the poster.

I think the poster is designed to appeal to all ages, young and old, male and female. The designer has chosen powerful images to say that this film will be a heroic story of bravery and brotherhood, as we heard in the persuasive speech before the battle, '*we band of brothers*'.

Based on the dramatic poster, I would like to see the film, because I think it sends out the message that it will be a modern performance of this play by Shakespeare and will be enjoyable for a modern film audience.

Paragraph 4
Introduces a new point about other sections of the poster.

Good organisation of paragraphs into different ideas. Excellent reference back to the words of the speech.

Closing paragraph
Strong summary statement to close the answer and reinforce points argued. Positive closing sentence.

Section B

Question 5
In your opinion, what elements of the text would engage listeners?

Tip

Purpose, style, tone, vocabulary, language and content are some **elements** of the text.

Sample answer
The purpose of the dramatic opening sentence is to shout out for audience attention, *People of Ireland*. This speaker wants a chummy relationship with listeners so he uses informal, ordinary words and phrases, e.g. *Listen up*. This is the confident, chirpy, friendly style of the TV frontman, who wants to create excitement in listeners. The style is dramatic and persuasive, but deliberately informal, e.g. *wannabe … get yourself down.*

The tone is lively and upbeat. The promise is excitement, fame and fortune, intended to persuade listeners that any ordinary Joe might become *the next big thing*. The message is appealing to people's desire for money and fame. Questions are used to excite reaction in people's heads, one coming very fast after the other. *Think you've got what it takes? Reckon you could be …?* The language is all hyperbole, *millions, dazzling, worldwide*. There is even some poetic technique in the alliteration we hear in *showcase* and *shine*.

The speaker is on a mission. His job is to persuade as many people as possible to pile in for the auditions. His words are carefully chosen to excite, impress and persuade *opportunity*, *conquer, shine*. The language he uses is dramatic, promising the things his audience would like to have, money, fame and success: *get ready to conquer the world*. The persuasion ends with a loud WOW and an exclamation mark.

Examiner's comment

Paragraph 1
There is clear focus on purpose, style and the language used in the text. The candidate's vocabulary to describe language style, *dramatic*, *persuasive*, *informal*, is impressive.

Paragraph 2
The answer moves to tone, makes a point and develops it with supporting quotation. The candidate demonstrates impressive knowledge of the correct terms for describing language. Upbeat, friendly, persuasive tone. Points out the use of **hyperbole** and **alliteration**.

Paragraph 3
Identifies the mission is to **engage** and persuade. The promise of money, fame and success. Every point made is supported by quotation or evidence from the text. Thoughtful comment on the words and the effective use of punctuation in the closing sentence

Question 6

Read this extract from the 1916 Proclamation.

Compare and contrast the purpose, language and style of this speech with the television script in question 5 on page 149.

Sample answer

This speech contrasts hugely with the television script in its content, its language and its style, but there is a similarity in its purpose which is to persuade. This is a *Proclamation* which declares that it is an official public announcement of a very important moment or event.

In language, it uses longer sentences and its words are heroic, which suits the style of the leader of a revolution. However, like the TV presenter, its purpose is to seize and hold people's attention. Something important is to be said and each of these speakers is calling for attention, although for very different purposes.

The Proclamation language is formal and dignified. It asks for the attention of all citizens, men and women. This speaker is not talking about money and success, but about history, tradition and patriotism. He uses solemn, impressive language; words such as *God*, *nationhood* and *freedom*. He says he speaks *in the name of God* and he says he speaks for Ireland, past and present.

Both speakers are on a mission. The aim in each case is to make people join in something, a TV show or a revolution. So both speakers are trying to persuade. The Proclamation speaker tells his countrymen and women that he has right on his side. He uses inspiring and dramatic phrases such as the phrase *summons her children to her flag*. There is the use of alliteration in *summons ... strikes* and in *flag ... freedom*.

Examiner's comment

Comment on each of the paragraphs in the sample answer opposite.

Paragraph 1

Paragraph 2

Paragraph 3

Final paragraph

Section C

Question 8

Remember that you have two tasks: First, to specify what appears on the poster (which could be a particular scene, a mixture of images and words, a collage, etc.); and second, to explain how your suggestions would create excitement about seeing the film.

Tip

You have studied two film posters – *The Glass Castle* on page 26, and *Henry V* on page 145. Study these images and the sample answers related to them to help you with this question.

Possible points could include:

setting (place, time of day or night), characters, words or phrases you might like to include, colours, light or shading (what mood do you want to create?), costumes, facial expressions, a tagline or slogan, and quotations.

Question 9

(a) definitely / principles

(b) knowledge / grammar / disappoint / embarrass

(c) rhythm / beginning / autumn

(d) government / necessary / achieve / success

(e) believe / deceived / receipt / ceiling

(f) principal / taught / behaviour

Sample Paper 3 – Change

Section A

Question 1

(a) How does the setting for this scene create mood or atmosphere?

Sample answer

Time and place are very important in **creating mood or atmosphere**. This scene happens at night, in the darkness of a **remote bogland** just after the shooting of two men. Everything is deathly quiet. The silence creates tension which is broken by a '**whispered**' question from the old woman. Noble is so nervous he cannot hold the match steady. Then there is the little light of a lamp and she repeats the same question.

The narrator goes out into the darkness and looks up at the stars. All he can hear is the sound of the birds '**shrieking**', and the '**mumbling**' of the old woman behind him. So we imagine the silent narrator at the door looking out and the two people behind him praying at the fireplace.

The darkness, the silence and the shrieking of the birds create a grim, eerie, nightmarish **atmosphere**. He describes the 'bloody stars' and 'the little patch of bog' that seemed 'a million miles away', and his terrible thoughts of the men they have buried in the remote bogland.

Examiner's comment

Shows understanding of the word 'setting' in the opening sentence, i.e. it means the time and the place.

Repeats the key words of the question in the opening sentence.

Uses information given in the background paragraph on the examination paper ('a remote bogland').

Excellent use of accurate quotation and detail from the text. Imaginative, creative response and ideas. Ideas are well organised in separate paragraphs.

(b) A key moment is a scene or moment of great emotional intensity that often illuminates character and makes a strong impact on the reader. In light of this definition, what aspects of this closing scene make it a key moment?

Sample answer

There is **great emotional intensity** in this scene, which we can imagine as the last dark scene at the end of a play. There are three characters, each one performing a role, shocked by what has just happened. The dramatic atmosphere, the whispered questions and abrupt answers, the little light of the lamp, the prayers, and especially the silent reflections of the narrator make it a key scene. The scene illuminates their characters, each responding in his or her own way.

It begins in pitch darkness with a tense whisper that startles Noble so much that the tiny light of a match goes out. The old woman heard a spade being put back, so she suspects that a grave has been dug. Her way of dealing with the situation is to ask angry questions.

In my opinion, the words '**by God**' are the start of the most moving key moment. We imagine the old woman and Noble falling to their knees in prayer while the narrator pushes his way out into the starlight and the '**shrieking of the birds**'. While they try to find consolation in prayer, the narrator just feels lost and lonely. His thoughts and desperate feelings create the strongest key moment, shedding light on his compassionate character and showing us his deepest self.

This scene shows us how a young man feels when he has just buried two men who have been shot before his eyes. He says he felt 'so strange', like he has never felt in his life before. His imagination is running riot. The grave is 'a million miles away' and the stars seem '**bloody**'. The **great emotional intensity** is in the way he describes his feelings:

'I was somehow very small and very lost and lonely.'

His character is changed forever more. He knows that something has happened that will change his life forever and he can never be the same person again. The last line says that this night has marked a turning point in his life, 'Anything that happened to me afterwards, I never felt the same about again.'

The scene makes a strong impact, in both its emotional intensity and its illumination of character. It makes us see the desperate atrocities that happen to ordinary people in war and the damage that war brings to people's lives.

Examiner's comment

Write the comments you would make commenting on good points in this answer. Remember **PIE** and **FIDOL** in making your comments.

Question 4

(a) Crankiness, being easily irritated or annoyed

(b) Made a sudden movement that showed nervousness or fear

(c) High-pitched loud screeching made by birds

(d) Muttering, speaking low sounds you can't make out

(e) Lost his way

Section B

Question 5

(a) Identify two digital elements used in the above screenshot from the Basketball Ireland website.

Some digital elements might be:

- The header
- Navigation bar
- The use of the logo
- The inclusion of images
- The news updates
- The option to contact the association
- The links to Twitter and Facebook
- The various buttons to tap for more information or drop-down boxes

(b) What impression of Basketball Ireland is made in this moment on their homepage and how is that impression communicated in both images and text?

Sample answer

Both in words and images, this page creates an impression of Basketball Ireland as a lively, dynamic, successful organisation with a lot going on and a lot to celebrate. It also shows in the image and in the words, 'Women's European Championship' that it is inclusive of male and female players. The side photograph shows a strong male player about to shoot into the net.

The screenshot celebrates success, '**History Makers – Ireland U18W storm into semi-final**'. The words are supported by the happy photograph of the moment of victory where you can see cheering crowds of supporters in the background.

The page also lets users know that there is more to find out by tapping buttons that give '**more news**' and '**latest results**'. The logo is prominent and the blue sky and clouds in the background give an impression of soaring to great heights.

Examiner's comment

Clear focus on the question in the opening paragraph. The student uses words and phrases from the question in the opening sentence.

The student gives equal attention to both images and text, not neglecting one or the other.

The student makes points quickly and briefly, having noted that this question only carries 10 marks.

Short paragraphs, each making brief, clear points.

Every point made is supported by quotation or evidence from the text.

Very strong final sentence.

Section C

Question 7

(a) Free and friendly conference

(b) It useth an enforced ceremony

(c) There are no tricks in plain and simple faith

(d) Speak your griefs softly

(e) Sell and mart your offices for gold

Question 8

(a) *Hollow men, like horses hot at hand / Make gallant show and promise of their mettle*

(b) *Or, by the gods, this speech were else your last*

(c) e.g. Are you forgetting why we assassinated Caesar? Each one of us who killed him believed that we were doing it for the cause of justice. Is one of us now going to corrupt our cause by taking bribes?

Question 10

You can see from this question how important it is to read and reread your key scenes. Be so prepared that you can picture the performance in detail on stage and know your quotations so that you quote accurately.

You have already done a lot of written preparation for this question in the *Responding to Shakespeare* section of this book.

It will help you to answer this question if you look back at the exam preparation work on pages 70–75.

Samples of High Quality and Medium Quality Answers

Responding to studied poems

What will I do?

You will put yourself into the mind of the examiner, reading sample answers and identifying the qualities that examiners look for in top-scoring writing.

What will I learn?

How to begin, how to proceed and how to complete a high quality answer.

The first step, before you put pen to paper, is to be clear about the task. Ask yourself the question:

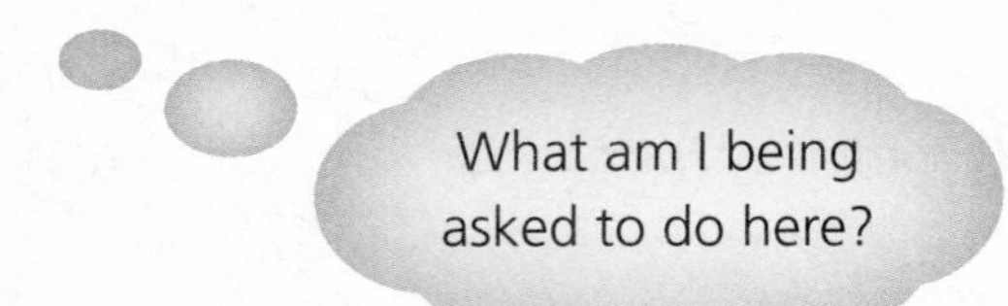

The next questions are:

How many parts are there in this question?

What are the key words or phrases in the question?

Mark the key words in the question.

Your first paragraph should include those key words, letting the examiner know that you have understood what you are being asked to do and that you will deal with the task.

As you finish each paragraph, go back to the paper and reread the question, asking:

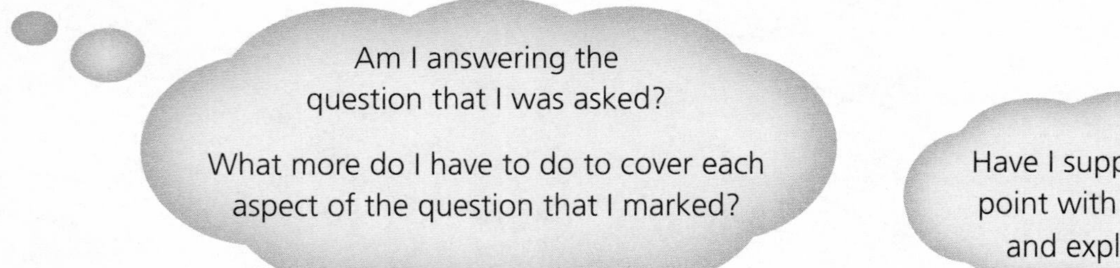

Have I supported each point with illustration and explanation?

Your task is to present creative, thoughtful ideas in logical sequence and in separate paragraphs.

If you have worked on your vocabulary by reading, then you will show the examiner that you have a good store of words to describe your responses to texts.

Finally, you will learn how to conclude an answer with a strong closing sentence. Why is this important? Because at that final moment, the examiner stops reading what you have written and awards your mark.

Examples in this section

In the examples that follow, each answer begins with a clear statement that tells the examiner that this candidate is on task, thinking clearly and deeply about the question. In each paragraph, points are supported by reference to or quotation from the text.

There are **20 marks** for each question.

Examination question

A poem may stay in our memories because of its appeal to our emotions and our senses.

Select a poem you have studied and explain how this statement applies to your understanding of this poem. Use the poem to support your ideas. (20 marks)

What am I being asked to do here? e.g.
I remember a poem because the feelings/ emotions and the sights/sounds/scents/images in it appealed to me.

Mark the separate aspects of the question that must be answered. Circle, highlight or underline the key words that you will deal with in your answer. If you leave out a key word, you will lose the marks for that part of the question.

A poem may (stay in our memories) because of its (appeal) to our (emotions) and our (senses).

The examiner will expect **use of the text as support for ideas** and will reward **clear, focused, well-expressed, well-developed and supported responses**.

Read the following two answers, and decide which is the high quality answer, and which is the medium quality answer.

Place the appropriate examiner's comments in the boxes opposite each sample answer.

In the sample answers, underline any inaccurate quotations or misspellings. Insert punctuation marks if they have been left out.

High-quality answer (mark range 19–20)	Medium-quality answer (mark range 12–18)
Clearly focused. From paragraph 1, it answers the question that was asked.	Loses focus – drifts into summary.
Interesting thoughts and ideas – ideas are developed, showing deep thinking and personal engagement with the poem.	Some good thoughts and ideas, but limited development and little personal engagement.
Clear and lively expression, good vocabulary.	Some flaws in expression.
Shows a strong, creative, imaginative response to the poem.	There is some creativity in the response.
Writing is well organised – ideas are presented in separate paragraphs.	The writing is organised in some respects.
The points made are well supported by quotation.	Inaccurate quotation.
Spelling and punctuation are very good.	Reasonably good spelling and punctuation.

Put yourself in the mind of the examiner.

In the text box provided alongside the answer, write appropriate phrases from the examiner's comments.

Sample answer A

Title of poem 'The Lake Isle of Innisfree'

Name of poet W.B. Yeats

The Lake Isle of Innisfree is my favourite poem. The title is the beautiful name of the island where Yeats loved to go on holidays when he was a child so it is full of emotion and happy memories. It makes a special appeal to the senses. The imagery and the alliteration in the sounds of the water and the crickets are very apealing.

In the first stanza he describes the little house he wants to build. He loves the peace and the sounds in the morning and the evening, 'evening full of the bird's wings.' In the second stanza, the colours and the description of night and day are very apealing and so is the quiet atmosphere. The stanza starts in the misty morning and finishes at night.

In my opinion the best stanza is the last because it is full of deep feeling and apeal to the sences. He repeats the first line 'I will arise and go now' but this time with deeper feeling of sadness because he is so far away and he feels far away and lost in the noisy city. He is standing on a grey road in London wishing he was in Innisfree listening to the water lapping. The greatest emotion of all is in the last line.

Sample answer B

Title of poem 'Stopping by Woods on a Snowy Evening'

Name of poet Robert Frost

I have chosen a poem that I will always remember because I love its dark, mysterious, wintry feelings, and its sights and sounds of snow and trees and frozen water. In this poem, as he describes snow falling on lonely woods, Robert Frost is also describing what he thinks and feels in his deepest self. The emotions and the senses go together. You see and hear what he sees and hears so strongly that you understand his feelings of cold, loneliness and a little fear.

On this 'darkest evening of the year,' he appeals to sound and sight with the tinkling of the 'harness bells,' 'the sweep of easy wind' and the expanse of 'woods and frozen lake.' In the eerie silence, he is almost hypnotised and lulled into not going any further. Far from other people, in the darkness and falling snow you imagine how solitary he is and how alone he feels in his thoughts like we all do at times. Then he hears the tinkling harness bells and decides to move on.

The alliteration helps the lines to stay in your memory; 'dark and deep' or 'sound's the sweep.' The clip-clop, musical rhythm of the rhymes, 'deep … keep … sleep' is also memorable. Most memorable of all is the strange emotion of the beautiful and mysterious last lines which say that he will not stay hypnotised by the frozen loneliness. Instead, he will continue his journey to the people, maybe his family, waiting for him at home,

'But I have promises to keep,

And miles to go before I sleep.'

Now it's your turn …

(You may, if you wish, choose to rewrite and improve the **medium quality** answer above. Raise it to **high quality** with better opening and conclusion, clearer organisation, more personal engagement, use of accurate quotation, improved expression, spelling and punctuation, etc.)

A poem may stay in our memories because of its appeal to our emotions and our senses.

Select a poem you have studied and explain how this statement applies to your understanding of this poem. Use the poem to support your ideas. (20 marks)

Title of your studied poem '________________________________'

Name of poet ________________________________

Imagine you are the examiner awarding a mark out of 20.

Use the wide margin to the side of your answer to write the comments that you think an examiner would make about your work.

N.B. There is a third category of **low quality** answers. If your answer is in this category, you are not writing at a Higher Level standard.

Low quality answer
Does not show understanding of the question or the task. Struggles to address what is asked.
Ideas are not clear and not relevant to the task. Shows little thought or reflection on the question.
Ideas are left undeveloped.
Points are not illustrated, explained or supported by accurate quotations.
There is no clear structure. The writing is disorganised and paragraphed.
The candidate's expression is poor, with many flaws. The register is inappropriate. The vocabulary is very limited.
There are significant errors in spelling and lack of correct use of punctuation marks.

Appreciating character – Responding to a Shakespearean soliloquy

Read the following speeches from Shakespearean plays.

1. The speech made by Henry to his army at Agincourt (page 141).
2. Polonius's advice to his son, Laertes, who is about to sail away from home (page 60).
3. Richard's soliloquy (page 65).

Reread both the **background** introduction and **Richard's soliloquy** on page 65.

Examination question

A Shakespearean soliloquy can be a key moment, revealing the innermost thoughts and feelings of a character to the audience.

Explain how this statement applies to your understanding of the opening soliloquy spoken by Richard. (20 marks)

Highlight, circle or underline the key words in the question that you will address in your answer.

A Shakespearean soliloquy can be a key moment, revealing the innermost thoughts and feelings of a character to the audience.

The examiner will highly reward clear, focused, well-expressed, well-developed and supported answers.

High quality answer (mark range 20–19)		Medium quality answer (mark range 18–12)	
High quality ideas and observations.		Low on ideas – more summary than thinking or analysing.	
Uses quotation to illustrate points made.		Limited use of quotation to illustrate points made.	
Ideas are developed.		Ideas are left hanging without development.	
Clear and lively expression, good vocabulary.		Flaws in expression, sentences do not flow when read aloud.	
Shows a strong, creative, imaginative response.		Some strength, but overall a response that lacks conviction or imagination.	
Writing is well organised – ideas are presented in separate paragraphs.		Writing is organised in some respects.	
Spelling and punctuation are very good.		Reasonably good spelling and punctuation.	

Read the two sample answers below, looking for evidence of the comments above. One of the answers is **high quality**, and the other is **medium quality**.

Write your comments on each of the sample answers **A** and **B**, using phrases from the comments, in the text box provided alongside the answer.

Sample answer A

Yes, I agree with this statement. This soliloquy is a key moment. It reveals the innermost thoughts and feelings of a character to the audience. It is summertime and peace has come after war. Everyone is enjoying themselves, but Richard tells us that he is unhappy and that he has secret plans. In the background note it says that he intends to murder his own brother.

His thoughts are all about how lonely and angry he feels at other people. He knows that women don't feel attracted to him and he seems very bitter about that. Even dogs bark at him when he passes by. He says, 'I cannot be a lover'. He also says he is determined to be the devil and he has evil plots. He will get his brother Clarence put into prison and then he will arrange his murder. His dream is to be king, whatever the cost. He will make other people hate each other the way he hates them,

'set my brother Clarence and the king
In deadly hate against each other'

He stops talking as soon as Clarence comes along. This is a key moment because now the audience knows a lot about Richard that other people in the story do not know. He has revealed thoughts and feelings in the soliloquy that he stops talking about when other people can hear him.

Sample answer B

Shakespeare gives a character a soliloquy when he wants to show the audience his deep, hidden self, the secret thoughts and emotions which are never spoken in public conversation. This is key to understanding a character. This opening soliloquy is a moment of truth, drama and revelation of character. It shows us that Shakespeare's soliloquies are a brilliant dramatic technique. Why? Because in this key moment, Richard reveals what he thinks and feels in his deepest, evil self.

It is a dramatic start to the action of the play, laying bare his evil ambition and his determination. More than that, it reveals that he has murderous plans, 'Plots have I laid.' Richard was so ambitious to be King that he murdered his own older brother so that he himself would get the throne. Because of this soliloquy, the audience will know Richard's character and what goes on in his mind, while other characters in the story will not.

The first eight lines are about the happiness everyone feels now there is peace, 'glorious summer.' Then comes Richard's twisted, bitter mind, 'But I …' He hates his appearance, 'Deform'd, unfinish'd.' He is not part of the peace celebrations, 'hate the idle pleasures of these days.' He feels like a lonely, bitter, despised outsider. Women are not attracted to him and even 'dogs bark at me.'

His revenge will be to seize power by becoming a murderer. 'I am determined to prove a villain.' Lastly, he tells us that he hides all these hateful, destructive thoughts and feelings inside himself. When he hears someone coming he says, 'Dive, thoughts, down to my soul.'

Expand your vocabulary of adjectives in preparation for the examination

From your reading of the three speeches, list five adjectives that describe each of these men. You have a selection of adjectives to describe Shakespearean characters on pages 200–201.

Remember!

You are allowed to use synonyms.

Henry V	Polonius	Richard

Showing critical appreciation – Beginnings and endings in poetry

Below are the opening and closing lines of five poems.

'Barbara Frietchie'	John Greenleaf Whittier
'Alisoun' from The Canterbury Tales	Geoffrey Chaucer
'The Responsibility'	Peter Appleton
'Jabberwocky'	Lewis Carroll
Sonnet 64	William Shakespeare

Read all the beginnings and endings and then answer the questions that follow.

Opening lines

A. 'Twas brillig, and the slithy toves
Did gyre and gimble in the wabe;

B. And she had plucked her eyebrows into bows,
Slenderly arched they were and black as sloes.*

C. I am the man who gives the word,
If it should come, to use the Bomb,

D. Like as the waves make towards the pebbled shore,
So do our minutes hasten to their end

E. Up from the meadows rich with corn,
Clear in the cool September morn,

Closing lines

1. And ever the stars above look down
On thy stars below in Frederick town!

2. All mimsy were the borogroves,
And the mome raths outgrabe.

3. High shoes she wore, and laced them to the top.
She was a daisy, O a lollipop!

4. And yet to times in hope my verse shall stand,
Praising thy worth despite his cruel hand.

5. I am the man behind it all;
I am the one responsible.

* Small blue-black sour fruit

1. For each of the three beginnings, select which of the endings (1, 2, 3, 4 and 5) you think is the correct one. Score **2 marks** for each correct answer.

Opening	Closing
A	
B	
C	
D	
E	

2. Justify your matches, based on two or more of **content**, **language**, **style**, **technique**, **rhyme**, **rhythm** or other **poetic features**.

Tip

Use these pointers to help you in this task.

Your aim is to show the examiner that you can identify a possible **theme** in a poem.

You should also be able to point out particular **techniques**.

Can you comment on the **style** of language to help you to match the openings and closings?

Say the lines to yourself to listen for **rhyme** and **rhythm**.

Can you see the poet's liking for **alliteration**, **assonance**, **imagery** or **rhyming couplets**?

Are the **words** long or short? Is there use of **repetition** to reinforce a word or phrase?

Write your own answers and then look at the sample answers on page 220.

Score **10 marks** for each answer.

3. Can you now match the poems to their authors and titles? Score **2 marks** for each correct answer.

Poem	Author and title
A	
B	
C	
D	
E	

Sample answers for this section

Appreciating character

Henry V		Polonius		Richard	
confident	self-assured	shrewd	anxious	wicked	malevolent
courageous	fearless	fatherly	irritating	scheming	nasty
inspiring	positive	careful	wary	underhand	secretive
strong	unafraid	cautious	worldly wise	evil	bad
charismatic	enthusiastic	clever	sharp	vicious	jealous
imaginative	eloquent	ambitious	astute	depraved	vile
				aggressive	violent

Showing critical appreciation

1.

Opening	Closing
A	2
B	3
C	5
D	4
E	1

2.

I have linked **A** and **2** based on its descriptive, imaginative, funky **language**; the **creative** words coined (invented) by the poet; the bizarre **imagery** of imaginary creatures 'gyring' and 'gimbling'; the jaunty **rhythm** in all four lines, and the fact that the **end words** 'toves / 'borogoves' and 'wabe / outgrabe' **rhyme.** These lines must have been written by the same poet.

I have linked **B** and **3** because they each describe a fashion-conscious girl's appearance. I notice when I count the beats in each line that there are exactly 10 beats, making a lilting, dancing **rhythm**, happy and fun-loving, like the fashionable girl herself. I see **assonance** also in 'And … and … black' and then again in 'laced … daisy …'

Both opening and closing lines are **rhyming couplets**. Both use **imagery**. The girl is compared with shiny dark fruit, flowers and a lollipop. The technique in the opening is a **simile**, 'black as sloes'. In the last line, the language is informal and funny, using **metaphor** as if he can't find enough similes to compare her with. The O in the middle of the line is unusual, followed by the exclamation mark, as if he's saying she's gorgeous, 'She was a daisy, O a lollipop!'

I have linked **C** and **5** for the simple **technique** of **repetition** in 'I am the man', but also for the **theme** of responsibility for the bomb. This poet uses **short**, **one-syllable words** when he wants the line to race along as if destruction is inevitable. You say the line fast because it trips along, 'I am the man who gives the word.'

The surprise slow halt comes with the longest, **four-syllable**, **word** which he keeps until the very last shocking moment. This is the heavy, long word, 'responsible'. You say it slowly so you know how important and destructive it is. The **language** in all four lines is solemn, **formal** and strict, like a military report.

D and **4** are linked by the use of **language** of the past, words that we no longer use. They are also similar in the use of **imagery** and **rhythm**. The **theme** in all four lines is time. The **simile** in the first two lines compares the passing of time with the breaking of waves, 'Like as ... waves ... so do our minutes ... end.'

The last lines **personify** time's 'cruel hand'. The **rhythm** is steady; you can count exactly **ten beats** in every line, just like you can in Shakespeare's plays. The **tone** in the opening is pessimistic and solemn; but this sad tone changes in the closing **rhyming couplet** to 'hope'. The **theme** is the sadness of time that brings life to an end, but the last lines say that a poem defeats time because it lives forever, 'And yet, to times in hope my verse shall stand.'

I have linked **E** and **1** because both use **descriptive language** and they sound like the beginning and ending of an old story**.** I see a link between the opening lines that look 'up' from the corn-filled meadows, while the closing lines 'look down'. The words 'morn' and 'thy' tell me that like **D**, this poem was written long ago. The poet likes rhyme, 'corn / morn' and 'down / town'.

The first lines describe a place where something important is about to happen. The last lines are written to God above. My guess is that a story has been told in **colourful**, **musical language**, and this story has something to do with the stars.

3.

Poem	**Author and title**
A	Lewis Carroll, 'Jabberwocky'
B	Geoffrey Chaucer, 'Alisoun' from *The Canterbury Tales*
C	Peter Appleton, 'The Responsibility'
D	William Shakespeare, Sonnet 64
E	John Greenleaf Whittier, 'Barbara Frietchie'

Common Errors

Students should be able to:

Use language conventions appropriately, especially … spelling.

(Final Exam Requirements: English Specification, 15)

Definition

A **convention** is a traditional or agreed way of doing something.

A **spelling convention** is an agreed correct spelling.

Spelling

Good spellers train themselves in three good habits.

1. As you prepare for this exam, **check** any spelling you have a doubt about. Do not attempt a difficult word and just hope it's correct.
2. When you find the correct spelling, **pause** a minute to **say** it aloud, **see** it with your eyes closed and **learn** it.
3. **Write** it down and say it aloud again.

Tip

Golden rule: Never allow a wrong spelling to become a repeat mistake in your answers.

Does the examiner deduct marks for mistakes in advanced vocabulary? ✔

The examiner will make allowances if you misspell a difficult, ambitious word; but you will lose marks for repeated misspelling of common words. ✔

How many marks might I lose for bad spelling? ✔

You can lose up to 10% of marks assigned to a question. ✔

As you work through this section, highlight or circle the spellings that you need to **check**, **cover**, **write**. This is the way to eliminate your spelling mistakes.

On a scale of **1–10**, circle the where you think you are on the 'good spelling scale'.

1	2	3	4	5	6	7	8	9	10
not very good									**extremely good**

Now circle the point that you think you could achieve in four weeks of regular practice (e.g. three 20-minute sessions each week), as part of your home study. Be ambitious but realistic – you'll have to stick to your promise, as we'll be checking up on your progress later!

Common homophones

1. Tick the box below that describes your ability to choose the correct spelling of these homophones.

Definition

Homophones are words that sound the same, but have different spellings depending on their meanings.

Homophone	Always correct	Sometimes correct	Never sure	Complete the phrase
allowed / aloud				Dogs not _______
bare / bear				_______ minimum
brake / break				Morning _______ studying
been / being				I have _______
by / bye / buy				_______ for now
cereal / serial				TV _______
coarse / course				Of _______ you can
dear / deer				_______ Sir
flour / flower				50 grams of _______
hear / here				I _______ you
heard / herd				You _______ me
its / it's				The car lost _______ wheels
knows / nose				He _______ it
knot / not				Tie this _______
patience / patients				_______ is a virtue
peace / piece				_______ of cake
principal / principle				Deputy _______
right / write				The _______ to vote
sight / site				Building _______
stationary / stationery				A _______ car
their / there / they're				No _______ not
to / too / two				It's _______ hot
weather / whether				Sunny _______
your / you're				No _______ not
who's / whose				_______ absent?

Give yourself **2** marks for each correct answer in the final column.

My score out of **50** is _____.

2. Write the two homophones in each case.

   a. There was a basket of **s**________**s** to greet us in the hotel **s**________.

   b. The **h**________ to the throne has fair **h**________.

   c. We had to **w**________ to be shown our correct **w**________ on the scales

   d. We were all **w**________ after a **w**________ without proper food.

   e. **S**________ people got the **s**________ right.

Give yourself **2** marks for each correct spelling.

My score out of **10** is _____.

3. Fit the correct homophone in the following sentences.

   Give yourself **1** mark for each correct answer.

   Then write in the definitions of the homophones to make sure you know what they mean.

   One example is done for you:

Who's leaving first?	**Whose** car is that?
Who's left that bag behind?	That's the girl **whose** phone was lost.
Who's coming with us?	I asked **whose** phone it was.
In 'who's', the apostrophe is used to replace the letters that have been left out in 'who is' or 'who has'.	You use 'whose' when something belongs to someone.

Aloud or allowed?

Under 18s are not __________	Read your poem __________
Guide dogs are __________	Sing the anthem __________
Definition:	Definition:

__/4

Bare or bear?

__________s growl in anger	Do the __________ minimum
Baby __________ cried	The walls were __________
I can't __________ that noise	Take the __________ essentials
Definition:	Definition:

__/6

Buy, by or bye?

__________ for now	Stand __________ me	__________ your own crisps
He waved good__________	He sped __________ us	__________ means purchase
Definition:	Definition:	Definition:

__/6

Dear or deer?

__________ Sir or Madam	Male __________ have antlers
Oh __________!	We saw a herd of __________
Definition:	Definition:

__/4

Coarse or course?

You're right, of __________	This blanket is __________
The __________ is finished	They're __________ and rude
Definition:	Definition:

__/4

Hear or here?

You __________ with your ears	__________ answers 'where?'
I __________ she's left	__________'s my new bag?
Definition:	Definition:

__/4

Nose or knows?

Who __________ if he'll arrive?	It's hard to draw a __________
My friend __________ Paris	Breathe through your __________
Definition:	Definition:

__/4

Knot or not?

The __________ was too tight	It's __________ happening
__________ is the speed of ships	Are you coming or __________?
Definition:	Definition:

__/4

Patience or patients?

I must practise __________	The __________ complained about the food.
__________ is a virtue	Nurses look after __________
Definition:	Definition:

__/4

Principle or principal?

Write to the school ________	Our head is a man of strong ________s
The ________ city is Kiev	It's against my ________s
Definition:	Definition:

__/4

Their, they're or there?

They forgot ________ togs	________ are two patients	________ late for lunch
They lost ________ patience	Look over ________	I'll go if ________ going
Definition:	Definition:	Definition:

__/6

My score out of **50** is _____.

Its and It's

Its shows possession. The horse stamped ***its*** hoof, the giraffe craned ***its*** neck, the cow swished ***its*** tail, the dog bared ***its*** teeth, the river burst ***its*** banks, the car lost ***its*** axle, etc.

It's shows that either the ***i*** in **it is** or the ***ha*** in **it has** has been left out.

It's (is) raining cats and dogs and ***it's*** (has) been like that all day long.

It's (is) no use saying you're sorry when ***it's*** (has) been a week since you scarpered off.

Fill in the words below; give yourself two marks for each correct answer.

1. The cat licked ________ paws.
2. ________ too hot to go out.
3. The club held ________ AGM.
4. The school got ________ gym.
5. ________ been very hard work.
6. ________ been a long day.
7. The dog wagged ________ tail.
8. ________ no use at all.

9. Don't tell me ________ over?

10. The horse broke ________ leg.

My score out of **20** is _____.

What is the the rule for *i* and *e* ?

I before E,

Except after C,

Or when sounded like A,

As in 'neighbour' and 'weigh'

I before E

Complete the following words. Give yourself **1** mark for each correct spelling.

1. Bel________ve
2. Fr________nd
3. Th________f
4. N________ce
5. Ch________f
6. Exper________nce
7. F________ld

Except after C

Complete the following words:

8. C________ling
9. Rec________ve
10. Rec________pt
11. Dec________ve
12. Dec________t

3. Or when sounded like A

Complete the following words:

13. N________ghbour
14. W________gh
15. Sl________gh
16. Th________r
17. Fr________ght
18. N________gh

19. V________l

20. ________ght (8)

My score out of **20** is ______.

Tip

Exceptions to the rule: science – weird – height.

Cover the page above and complete the following words. Give yourself **1** mark for each correct spelling.

I bel________ve that n________ghbours should be fr________nds. When our aunt________'s c________ing collapsed due to the w________ght of a treadmill and a toy Santa sl________gh on th________r upstairs landing, ________ght people who had heard the roars and shr___ks came in to help.

My score out of **10** is ______.

When to use 'practice' and 'practise'

'Practice', with a c, is a noun. 'Practise', with an s, is a verb. One way to remember this is that 'noun' comes before 'verb' in the dictionary, just as c comes before s in the dictionary.

So the noun is **practice**, e.g. the dentist's practice; practice makes perfect; you will get better at writing through daily practice.

The verb is **practise**, e.g. practise writing good opening sentences; she practised her song all day; he went out to practise his football skills.

Cover the page above and complete the following words.

Give yourself **2** marks for each correct spelling.

The doctor, who had her practi___e near the golf club, practi___ed her golf swing every evening, while her son went to basketball practi___e. Her husband was practi___ing for indoor five-a-side, so they had a sign saying 'Practi___e Makes Perfect' on their kitchen wall.

My score out of **10** is ______.

I-O-U

Rewrite in each word below in full, adding the letters I, O and U.

Give yourself **2** marks for each correct spelling.

Remember!

Remember 'I-O-U' for the following commonly misspelt words.

1. Wants to succeed — Ambit ___ ___ ___ s
2. Feeling tense or worried — Anx ___ ___ ___ s
3. Awful, dreadful, terrible — Atroc ___ ___ ___ s
4. Would like to know something — Cur ___ ___ ___ s

5. Tastes good — Delic ___ ___ ___ s

6. Really angry — Fur ___ ___ ___ s

7. It's clear to see — Obv ___ ___ ___ s

8. Important, not fun — Ser ___ ___ ___ s

9. Seems dodgy, needs investigation — Suspic ___ ___ ___ s

10. Believes in bad luck or the unexplainable — Superstit ___ ___ ___ s

My score out of **20** is ______.

58 tricky spellings

Word	Remember	Word	Remember
Accommodation	double **C**, double **M**	Achieve	**I** before **E**
Across	think **A** and **CROSS**	Appear	think **APP** and **EAR**
Autumn	ends in **MN**	Basically	ends in **ICALLY**
Beginning	double **N** before the **ING**	Believe	there is a **LIE** in be**LIE**ve
Business	remember **SIN**	Calendar	remember **A E A**
Cemetery	3 **E**s – EEEK!	Character	2 **C**s, 2 **A**s, 2 **R**s and an unexpected **H**!
Coming	lose the **E**	Completely	Compl**ETE** the word by adding **LY**
Conscience	ends in **SCIENCE**	Definitely	say **AYE** in defin**I**tely
Describe	remember **E I E**	Disappear	1 **S**, 2 **P**s
Disappoint	1 **S**, 2 **P**s	Embarrass	double **R**, double **S**
Especially	double **L**	Exaggerate	remember **AGGER** Mick Jagger swaggers exaggeratedly!
Experience	**I** before **E**	February	2 **R**s
Finally	double **L**	Forty	begins with **FOR** not **FOUR**
Friend	**FRI** is the friendly **END** of the week	Government	remember **NM**
Grammar	2 **M**s, 2 **R**s, 2 **A**s and a **G**	Happened	double **P**, single **N**
Height	unusually **E** before **I** and **GHT**	Immediately	double **M** and remember **ATELY**

Word	Remember	Word	Remember
Independent	3 **E**s	Intelligent	double **L** and ends in **GENT**
Interrupt	double **R**	Knowledge	2 words: **KNOW** and **LEDGE**
Loneliness	**Y** changes to **I**	Making	lose the **E**
Library	2 **R**s	Length	remember **GTH**
Meat	**EAT MEAT**	Necessary	**N**ever **E**at **C**hips **E**at **S**ensible **S**alads **A**lways (**R**eally **Y**ummy!)
Occasion	2 **C**s, 1 **S**	Peace	pe**A**ce not w**A**r
Piece	**I** before **E**, or a **PIE**ce of **PIE**	Principal	the principal is your **PAL**
Probably	don't forget the **A**	Queue	2 **U**s, 2 **E**s
Receive	**E** before **I**	Rhythm	**R**hythm **H**elps **Y**our **T**wo **H**ips **M**ove
Sentence	3 **E**s, 1 **C**	Sincerely	2 words: **SINCE** and **RELY**
Stationary	to stay still is to be **ST**ation**A**r**Y**	Stationery	think **E** for **E**nvelope
Strength	remember **LENGTH**	Together	**TO GET HER**
Wednesday	say it in 3 parts: **WED-NES-DAY**	Until	only 1 **L**

Partner up and take turns in asking each other 10 spellings from the list.

Each person holds the chart and asks 10 spellings. Then switch over. You will each be asked 20 spellings in total.

Tick off each spelling as you call it out.

Give yourselves **2** marks for each correct spelling.

My score out of **40** is ______.

Tip

Say or *write* the spelling you are asked for. Some people prefer to say. Others can only spell the word if they write it down.

Revision

Remember that at the beginning of this section, you gave yourself a mark on a scale of 1–10 for spelling.

You also said you would give four weeks of regular timed visits to this section (e.g. three 20-minute sessions each week), as part of your home study.

Having studied the full section and done your four weeks of regular time for spelling, now place yourself on the scale again.

On a scale of 1–10 (10 being *extremely good*), circle your place on the spelling scale:

1	2	3	4	5	6	7	8	9	10
not very good									**extremely good**

Tip

Arrange for someone to test you on *any* page when you have completed this section.

In each case, ask the person to test you on 10 words and to give you your score.

Answers

Common Homophones

1. Dogs not **allowed**; **Bare** minimum; Morning **break**; I have **been** studying; **Bye** for now; TV **serial**; Of **course** you can; **Dear** Sir; 50 grams of **flour**; **I hear** you; You **heard** me; The car lost **its** wheels; He **knows** it; Tie this **knot**; **Patience** is a virtue; **Piece** of cake; Deputy **principal**; The **right** to vote; Building **site**; A **stationary** car; No **they're** not; It's **too** hot; Sunny **weather**; No **you're** not; **Who's** absent

2. a. sweets / suite; b. heir / hair; c. wait / weight; d. weak / week; e. some / sum

Its and it's

1. The cat licked **its** paws; 2. **It's** too hot to go out; 3. The club held **its** AGM; 4. The school got **its** gym; 5. **It's** been very hard work; 6. **It's** been a long day; 7. The dog wagged **its** tail; 8. **It's** no use at all; 9. The horse broke **its** leg; 10. Don't tell me **it's** over?

I before E

1. Believe; 2. Friend; 3. Thief; 4. Niece; 5. Chief; 6. Experience; 7. Field; 8. Ceiling; 9. Receive; 10. Receipt; 11. Deceive; 12. Deceit; 13. Neighbour; 14. Weigh 15. Sleigh; 16. Their; 17. Freight; 18. Neigh; 19. Veil; 20. Eight

I **believe** that **neighbours** should be **friends**. When our **auntie's ceiling** collapsed due to the **weight** of a treadmill and a toy Santa **sleigh** on **their** upstairs landing, **eight** people who had heard the roars and **shrieks** came in to help.

When to use 'practice' and 'practise'

The doctor, who had her **practice** near the golf club, **practised** her golf swing every evening, while her son went to basketball practice. Her husband was **practising** for indoor five-a-side, so they had a sign saying '**Practice** makes Perfect' on their kitchen wall.

I-O-U

1. Ambitious; 2. Anxious; 3. Atrocious; 4. Curious; 5. Delicious; 6. Furious; 7. Obvious; 8. Serious; 9. Suspicious; 10. Superstitious

Expand your Vocabulary

Read this telephone conversation between James Herriot, the local vet, and Mr Pickersgill. It is taken from the James Herriot novel *Let Sleeping Vets Lie*.

Mr Pickersgill obviously had a comical problem with words, but this kind of confusion is not a good way to go through life. Check the pronunciation and meaning of any new words you encounter. Then add them to your vocabulary. As time goes by, you will accumulate a good selection of words to choose from. Then can you hit the right word that communicates what you want.

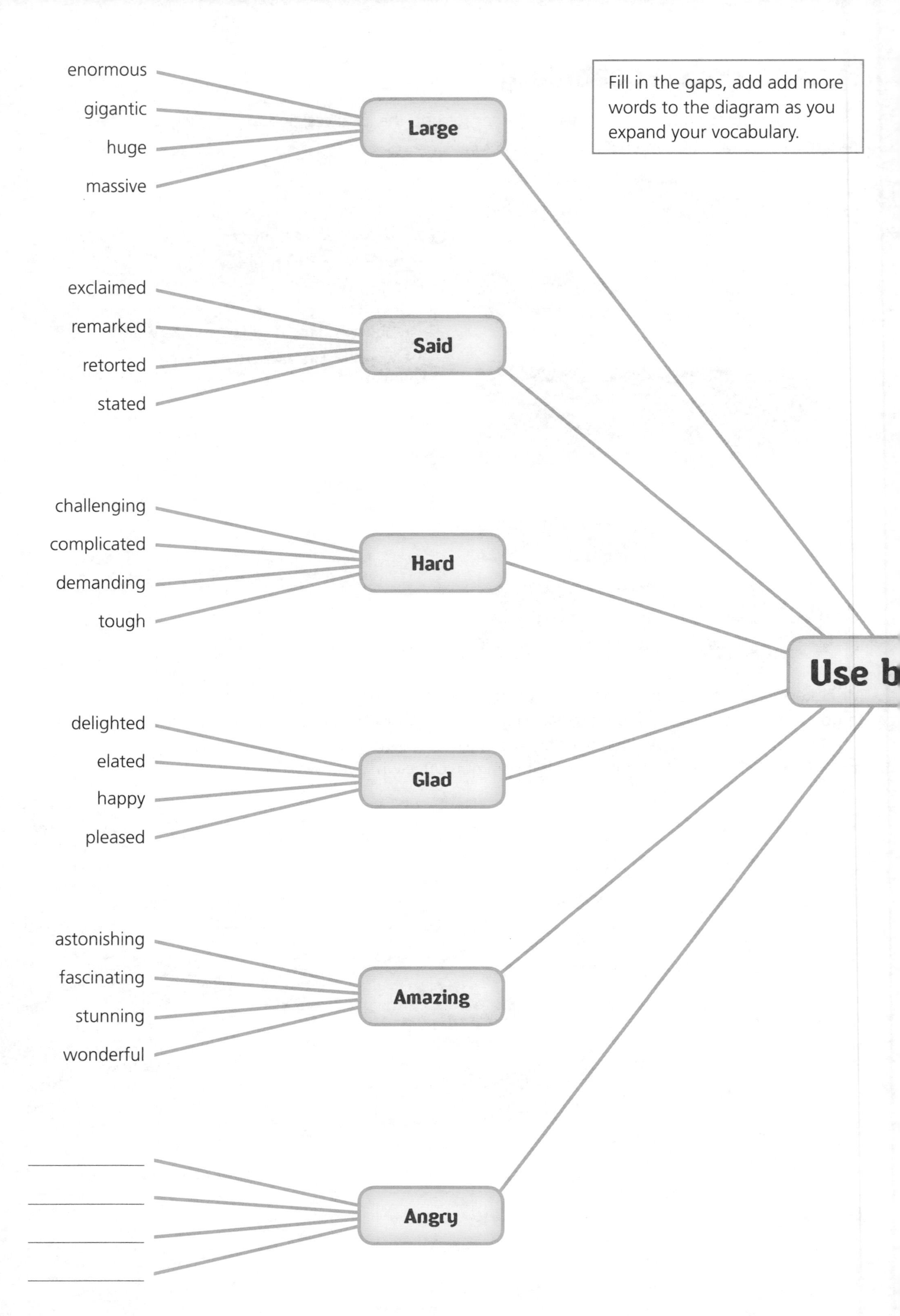
enormous
gigantic
huge
massive
Large
Fill in the gaps, add add more words to the diagram as you expand your vocabulary.
exclaimed
remarked
retorted
stated
Said
challenging
complicated
demanding
tough
Hard
Use b
delighted
elated
happy
pleased
Glad
astonishing
fascinating
stunning
wonderful
Amazing
Angry

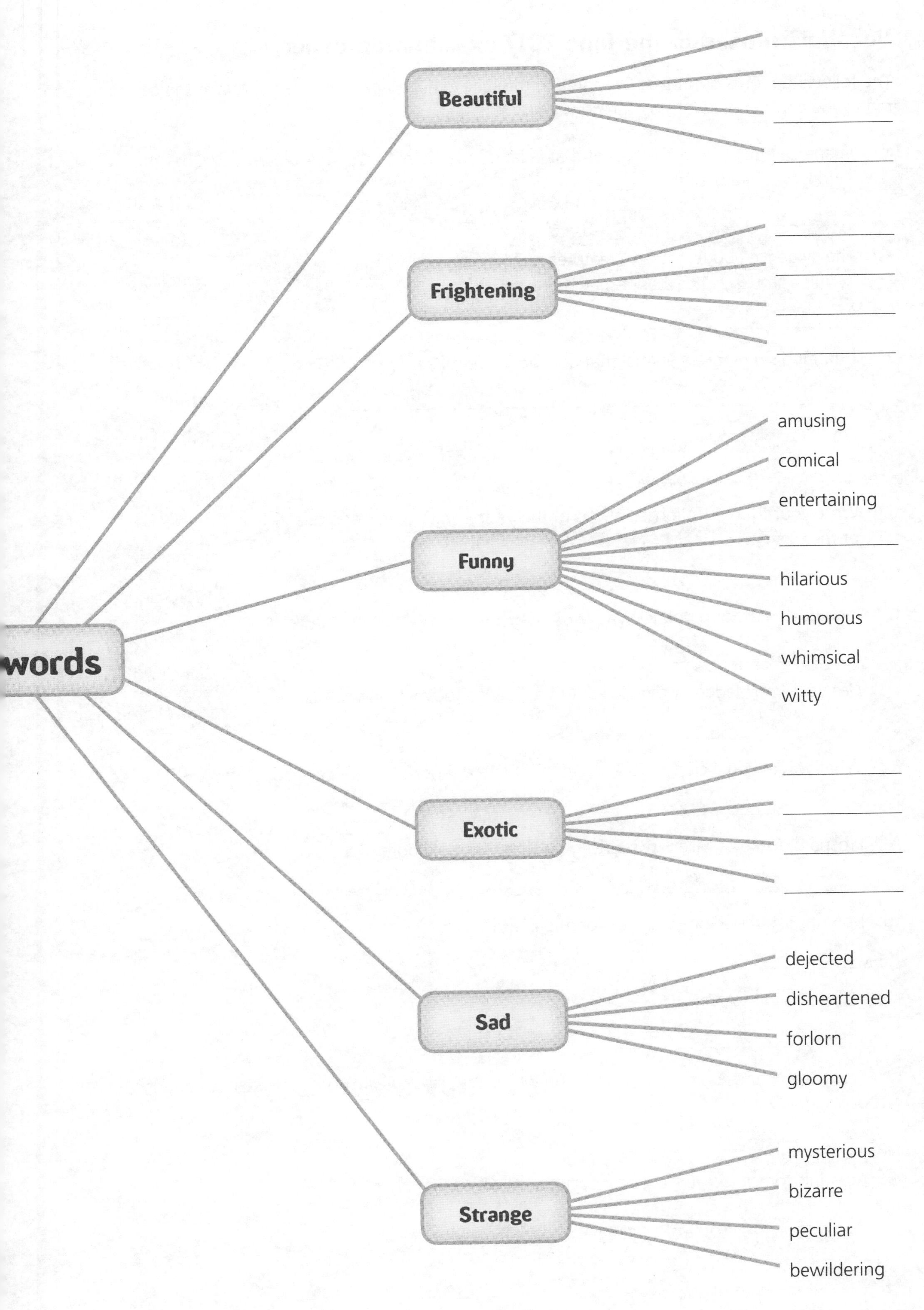
words
Beautiful
Frightening
Funny
amusing
comical
entertaining
hilarious
humorous
whimsical
witty
Exotic
Sad
dejected
disheartened
forlorn
gloomy
Strange
mysterious
bizarre
peculiar
bewildering

Vocabulary used in the June 2017 examination paper

The following words or phrases appeared in the June 2017 examination paper. Match the descriptions in red to the appropriate word on the right.

1. Shane Dunphy tries to find proof that Ireland's monsters that appear in folk tales really exist

   ____________________; ____________________

2. The evidence about mystery creatures is either legendary or based on people's stories rather than research or hard facts.

   ____

3. Haunting shriek of an animal that cannot be identified.

   ____________________; ____________________

4. I'm not easily convinced.

   ____

5. Write your thoughtful observations of the interesting aspects and qualities of the poster.

   ____

6. Identify at least two poetic creative or imaginative ways of using language.

   ____

7. Use your knowledge of the play to give evidence for your viewpoints.

   ____

8. What would you include in the poster to create a sense of excitement about what will happen?

   ____

9. Prospero, Duke of Milan, was driven out from his Dukedom.

   ____

10. He finds shelter and a safe place on the island.

    ____

11. Antonio is with Alonso.

    ____

12. Study the image composed of words, in which the size of each word indicates its frequency or importance.

    ____

13. An adult comes face-to-face in a hostile way with a teenager.

    ____

Confronts
Endeavours
Refuge
Mythical
Expelled
Sceptical
Justify
Critical analysis
Anticipation
Anecdotal
Techniques
Word cloud
Unidentifiable
Screech
In the company of